ARCHITECTURE IN THE AGE OF HUMAN–COMPUTER INTERACTION

This book investigates the spaces where architecture and computer science share a common set of assumptions and goals, using methods and objectives from architecture, ethnography, and human–computer interaction (HCI).

Architecture and HCI depend on and borrow from each other, and even share some vocabulary in their divergent disciplinary agendas. The authors here unpack the past, present, and potential futures of architecture and the user interface, employing the lens of ethnography and ethnographic practices to launch this exciting cross-disciplinary inquiry. The goal is the creation of an interface that is able to connect the wide range of embodied architectural space, the modes of interaction afforded by computation, and the social process of creating meaningful places.

This will be of great interest to upper-level students and academics in the fields of architecture, human–computer interaction, and ethnography.

Eric Sauda is a registered architect and Professor of Architecture at University of North Carolina at Charlotte (UNC Charlotte), United States of America. He specializes in the use of digital and computational technologies and their transformative effect on architecture.

Alireza Karduni is Assistant Professor of Human-Centered Computing at Simon Fraser University, School of Interactive Arts and Technology, Canada. His research lies at the intersection of human–computer interaction, data visualization, and thinking with data.

Donna Lanclos is an anthropologist and Senior Research Fellow in the Technology Enhanced Learning department at Munster Technological University, Ireland.

ARCHITECTURE IN THE AGE OF HUMAN–COMPUTER INTERACTION

Eric Sauda, Alireza Karduni, and Donna Lanclos

Routledge
Taylor & Francis Group
LONDON AND NEW YORK

Designed cover image: Cover Design: Alireza Karduni,
Cover Image: Chris Campbell

First published 2025
by Routledge
4 Park Square, Milton Park, Abingdon, Oxon OX14 4RN

and by Routledge
605 Third Avenue, New York, NY 10158

Routledge is an imprint of the Taylor & Francis Group, an informa business

British Library Cataloguing-in-Publication Data
A catalogue record for this book is available from the British Library

ISBN: 978-1-032-42593-1 (hbk)
ISBN: 978-1-032-42592-4 (pbk)
ISBN: 978-1-003-36339-2 (ebk)

DOI: 10.4324/9781003363392

Typeset in Optima
by SPi Technologies India Pvt Ltd (Straive)

CONTENTS

FIGURES

ACKNOWLEDGMENTS

This book is the result of a long collaboration between the authors, each bringing a different perspective to the work. It began with a curiosity about the ways in which the use of computers might be changing architecture – not just as faster tools for traditional methods, but rather how it might be changing our understanding of the limits and possibilities of architecture. This book focuses in particular on how changes in the emerging field of computer science, primarily around human–computer interaction, are happening at the same time. Anyone familiar with these trends may well suspect they are related.

The seduction of new technology can be difficult to resist, even if one suspects its impact may be overblown by its advocates. New technology has arrived before and, while it changes things, it never changes *everything*. But the only thing more problematic than messianic optimism is hidebound conservatism, the insistence that all important things are just as they were 10 years ago, 100 years ago, 1000 years ago.

The goal of this book then is to see how things change and how contemporary culture adapts to new circumstances when faced with what Marshall McLuhan described as a "new extension of man."

Much of this work has been advanced through a series of graduate seminar courses in the Design Computation Dual Masters degree program in Architecture and Computer Science at UNC Charlotte. The students brought enthusiasm and energy to these courses and enabled the testing of strategies and methods for the incorporation of data analysis in the study of spatial settings. The authors wish to thank Anna Anklin, Chelsea Hansen,

Kacie Ward, Richard Crouch, Chi Zhang, Xunxun Zhang, Janette Billings, Josn Kieb, Marc Remesi, Heather Tarney, Phillip Broszkiewics, Ashley Damiano, Bradford Guillet, Alex Shuey, Benjamin Sullivan, Fernando Claudio Rodriquex, Ashkan Radnia, Noushin Radnia, Alireza Fatemi, Nick Rawlings, and Atefeh Mahdavi Goloujeh. Graduate research assistantships from the Graduate School at UNC Charlotte provided us with strong support to advance our work. They were vital to our effort and deserve much credit for their contribution.

The authors also must thank our colleagues in both architecture and computer science for the many discussions and critiques of the ongoing work. It is one of the great joys of working in a university. Dr. William Ribarsky provided the widest perspective of visualization and data analysis and was an inspiration for our work. Dr. Wenwen Dou, Dr. Remco Chang, Dr. Caroline Ziemkiewicz, Dr. Isaac Cho, Dr. Charles Davis, Dr. Richard Souvenir, Dr. Scott Spurlock, Dr. Mary Lou Maher, and Dr. John Gero were at different stages of our research able to give us vital feedback.

All three authors want to acknowledge the excitement of working on this project together. The differences in our disciplines and training made it challenging but it forced a clarity of thought.

Alireza Karduni wishes to thank his parents, Vahideh Gandomikal and Habibollah Kardooni, for their patience, especially during the time spent on this book, for which they did not see their son for eight years. He would also like to thank his siblings Hoda, Neda, and Roozbeh Kardooni who supported him throughout. The work on this book occurred while working at UNC Charlotte, Northwestern University, IDEO, and finally and currently at Simon Fraser University, Canada. The mentorships, friendships, and experiences gained through these institutions were integral to the development of this work. Special thanks is deserved for the Simon Fraser University, School of Interactive Arts and Technology family who provided enough flexibility to work on this book in the very first few months of working at SIAT. Finally, he would like to thank his friends and family in Iran and other parts of the world, who through many hours of voice chats on Discord and online games, helped him get through the loneliness of immigration.

Eric Sauda wishes to thank Blain Brownell, the Director of the School of Architecture at UNC Charlotte for his help in arranging at very short notice a reassignment of duty that provided time that was invaluable to the research and writing of this book. And he most especially wants to thank his wife Georgette who in every way supported me during my entire career and especially during the hard labor of completing this book.

Donna Lanclos would like to thank her co-authors, Eric and Ali, for inviting her to be a part of this project. Itis hard sometimes to be in rooms, as an independent scholar, where you get to have the kind of conversations that eventually result in books. She is most grateful for them as colleagues and friends, for the conversations, and relieved at the completion of our book.

PREFACE

In 2004, Blockbuster Video operated more than 9,000 stores both in the USA and across the world. These stores employed 60,000 people and controlled 45% of the video rental market. The trip to a Blockbuster store, the stroll down the aisles, and the search for a video on Friday and Saturday nights was an integral part of life for millions of users. In 2010, Blockbuster declared bankruptcy and was down to 500 stores, and its share of the video rental market has shrunk from 45 to 3%; it has since disappeared altogether.

Ironically, in 2000, Netflix had offered to sell to Blockbuster its new service model that delivered DVDs directly to consumers by mail, using an internet site for browsing, sales, and scheduling. They were turned down cold.

Meanwhile, Netflix, as its name suggested from the beginning, has continued to develop its online presence. Based on improvement in network speed, information theory, and video content software, they were able to move quickly into delivering streaming content through the internet that does away with not just the architectural setting of the store but the physical artifact of the DVD. The search and the stroll had become virtual.

While it is a stretch to claim any exalted architectural status for Blockbuster stores (although it does bear an ironic resemblance to a *passeggiata* in Italy), it is clear that in this case at least, the physical has been replaced by the virtual. It is cold comfort to Blockbuster that to a considerable extent it had itself replaced movie theaters, and that Netflix itself is under intense pressure from competitors, both legal and illegal. Bits will be bits.

"I can't take it anymore," Marc Andreessen wrote suitably enough on his blog in 2008 (blog.pmarca.com). "I hereby inaugurate my *New York Times* Deathwatch, which will continue until the last Sulzberger has left the building."[1] Andreessen was founder of Netscape, one of the earliest startups in silicon valley, which he later sold for $4.6 billion. He founded two other startups, began the leading technology focused venture capital firm Andreessen/Horowitz and was an instrumental early board member on Facebook. Andreessen was also an unofficial spokesman for the ethos of Silicon Valley.

He was certainly right that the spread of online information and advertising had radically changed the newspaper business. Classified ads largely focused on automobiles and real estate and had been a reliable source of income for newspapers, but they had come close to vanishing. Craigslist, eBay, and later other sites including Zillow absorbed all available classified advertising. In addition, the emergence of social media allowed users to gather online in groups of any size, in effect competing with the large aggregated markets of traditional newspapers either directly or through the creation of many splintered audiences.

Andreessen presents his case as a zero-sum game. Either the newspaper will survive or it will be replaced. The function of new technology is to disrupt markets, behavior, and social institutions and replace them with new and better ones.

The current health of the *New York Times* then comes as something of a surprise. It employs a record number of journalists and while it has slightly fewer paper subscribers (800,000), it now has over 8 million digital subscribers and is showing healthy profits. While this was a difficult transition it was not, it turns out, a death watch. The institution adapted to a networked presence and thrived not as a social medium in any normal sense of the term but rather as a hybrid medium.

Kevin Kelley, founding Executive Editor of *Wired* magazine, is a leading editorial proponent of digital culture and experience. In 2006 he wrote an article (ironically in the *New York Times*[2]) outlining his understanding of books in general and libraries specifically. He begins by reporting on Google's project to digitize every book ever written and then proceeds to discuss the legal and intellectual rights issues, the accelerating hardware capabilities, and the advantages of digital formats, allowing for automated search and retrieval. He proposes this virtual library as a long time dream of humans dating back at least to Alexandria and which is finally achievable. He also imagines the role of physical books and architectural libraries as atavistic. As one of us is by profession keenly aware, libraries are not only (or even primarily) repositories for books. Just as important is the physical and social setting for gathering, collaborating, and researching.

The naive belief in the digital future imagines a dialectic battle between the old and the new, widely believed to be inevitably won by the future. And not by some mysterious, distant force but rather, as Alan Kaye of the Palo Alto Research Center implied, as "the best way to predict the future is to invent it." In this book we recognize the aggressive spirit abroad in Silicon Valley and its belief in a brave new world emerging through technology. Architecture and human–computer interaction now share an interest in buildings, in how people occupy buildings, and in what buildings mean to people.

Architecture's interest dates back thousands of years, although not in the form that we would necessarily recognize today. Evidence from the oldest book on architecture by Vitruvius shows it included engineering and even military fortification, although modern usage focuses only on building. As we will see in Chapter 2, architects recently have eagerly adopted computational methods mostly focusing on digital design and manufacturing, often involving complex and novel geometries. They also have come to share an interest in design as a method.

Computer science's interest is much more recent following the sequential resolution of foundational issues including programming, data structures, algorithms, and operating systems. Exemplified by the articulation of ubiquitous computing as an idea in the 1990s, an idea became common that computers would be found everywhere and in everything. This led not solely to buildings as a focus, but certainly they became a very prominent setting.

The focus in architecture is on the originality of a single building. Architecture is a one-at-a-time discipline, striving to create a unique building tuned to a specific context. It is rare to find a prominent architect who cites work by other architects except in the most cursory way (unless separated by considerable historical distance). By contrast, computer science is always focused on thousands or millions of examples or users collected over time. And computer scientists always include an extensive discussion of previous work (most of it recent) that form the foundation of new work.

Architecture is usually an attempt to create a balance of many factors. While a particular building often emphasizes one aspect of the design, they are typically described as "holistic," that is, including their construction, structure, human settings, energy consumption, and political/cultural meanings. Computer science is often a narrower emphasis on a specific technology and its application in one part of a built environment, for example augmented reality.

These differences are the context for this book. This Preface sets the stage for an emerging domain shared by architecture and human–computer interaction. As pressing and fruitful as this overlap may be, their respective interests are quite distinct. It is possible to keep both disciplines separate but if the goal is to imagine the emergence of a new hybrid, articulating and navigating these differences is required.

Notes

1 https://money.cnn.com/2008/02/21/news/newsmakers/quittner_andreessen.fortune/index.htm.
2 Johnson, Steven. "Scan This Book!" The New York Times Magazine, May 14, 2006. https://www.nytimes.com/2006/05/14/magazine/14publishing.html.

1

INTRODUCTION

Theory and Design in the First Machine Age is Reyner Banham's (1980) history of modern architecture from 1900 to 1930 and its fascination with new technological developments in the first machine age, including planes, cars, steamships, and factories. At the very end of the Conclusion, he offers this warning:

> The theorists and designers of the First Machine Age … were for allowing technology to run its course, and believed that they understood where it was going, even without having bothered to acquaint themselves with it very closely. In the upshot, a historian must find that they produced a Machine Age architecture only in the sense that its monuments were built in a Machine Age, and expressed an attitude to machinery – in the sense that one might stand on French soil and discuss French politics and still be speaking English.
>
> (p. 329)

Now, contemporary architects have become enamored of the design possibilities offered by computational methods. There is nothing unusual about this; architects have always shared or borrowed methods from other fields to accomplish their goals: statics from physics, deconstruction from philosophy,[1] precedent studies from art history,[2] modeling from descriptive geometry, sound from acoustics, human behavior from psychology and sociology, aesthetics from art.

DOI: 10.4324/9781003363392-1

This particular interest in computation has been reflected both in practice and in theory. In architectural practice, research on what became known as building information models (BIM) began around 1970, and by 2000, was widely adopted in the architecture and construction industries. BIM is a software system that uses digital representations of physical and functional characteristics of places that can be used in the design, construction, operation, and maintenance of buildings.

Computational methods have also been used for the exploration of innovative design. This has been engaged in various ways, ranging from the incorporation of features or devices associated with computer science such as displays, computer vision, and augmented reality into architectural designs as well as the application of sophisticated modeling largely borrowed from animation software such as FORMZ or product design software such as CATIA. This use of these more and more sophisticated methods has increased rapidly,[3] but the traffic in methodology has been one-sided. For example, we can see the influence that NURBS modeling has had on architecture form, but the architectural results have had little or no influence on the underlying geometric methods or on computer science.

But more recently, architectural theorists see computation not just as techniques like calculus borrowed from mathematics or models such as biomimicry borrowed from biology, but as a new and critical part of a contemporary theoretical structure of the discipline.[4] Architects are of course entitled to construct their own theories and to refer to what they wish from other fields, but as Banham reminds us in his critique of the development of "modern" architecture exactly one century ago, it is no simple matter to find common ground between architecture and technology.

Our goal in this book, then, is to understand the development of theory and practice in both architecture and computer science and to identify areas of common interest. These areas of common interest are beyond computer graphics and computer aided drawing (CAD) tools that are widely used by architects. We believe that both disciplines have been addressing overlapping issues centered on what is called embodied interaction. Human–computer interaction (HCI) design is for interaction in a specific spatial and human setting and in architecture design is to create interactive settings incorporating digital technologies in architectural settings.

It is worth noting as we begin this work that architecture and computer science have to this point very different histories and definitions for practice and theory. Architecture makes a plausible claim to thousands of years of history while computer science (and in particular HCI) has only existed since the 1970s. Computer science departments have been very flexible in adapting their research agenda to match the developing status and needs of computers in society. For example, shading algorithms that determine how light and color interact with the surfaces of 3D objects in computer graphics were actively researched beginning in the 1980s but by 2010 the issues were largely settled and the field moved on.

The idea of theory in each field has a different meaning. In computer science, theory can either be considered theoretical computer science derived from mathematics, or in less common cases such as computational ontology an adaptation of a philosophical term to a process of naming and defining the concepts, data, and entities of a domain. Theory in architecture has a much wider scope, and has shown considerable variation over time. It has sometimes been a straightforward guide to practice and at other times purposely constructed as an alternative to practice.

The proliferation of computers, and their embedding into everyday life, has created a greatly expanded new audience and the need to develop new ways to engage users from a wide variety of backgrounds and abilities. In 1955, there were a total of only 250 digital computers in the world. By 2013 it was estimated that the total number of computers worldwide was 1.5 billion,[5] counting only general-purpose computers and ignoring for the moment computers built into watches, phones, cars, refrigerators, and any number of other devices. At least 95.2% of all households in the USA have a personal computer. Early research on computers in electrical engineering focused on developing hardware and software systems, including prominently the graphic and display technologies, the rapid shrinking of central processing units, the exponential expansion of memory systems, and the application of formal systems to create programming languages and a wide variety of algorithms. The emergence of computer science as an academic discipline distinct from electrical engineering or mathematics is coincident with the emergence of the personal computer in the 1970s. The audience for computer science expanded from a small group of advanced scientists seeking solutions to difficult but well-defined problems to a broad and diverse audience. This emergence of HCI has led to a new focus on psychological and ethnographic methods and understandings in computer science.[6]

And the shift to human-centered design in HCI has led to an interest in collaboration with social scientists capable of bringing insights about how people are likely to understand and use the newly omnipresent machines. In both cases the potential has been largely untapped: in architecture because of a structural and professional myopia to the serious study of how people inhabit, value, and create place; and in HCI largely because behavioral observations have been used to find quick insights to design factors. Ethnography, a methodology for observing, analyzing, and representing human behavior and cultural systems, is pivotal to understanding both fields of architecture and HCI. Human occupation emerges as a key factor distinguishing architecture and engineering since their divorce during the Enlightenment. The development of ethnographic methodologies, particularly within the discipline of anthropology, provides avenues to generate in-person, open-ended, and "thick" descriptions of place, behavior, and meaning.[7] This is a turn from quantitative measures to qualitative understandings. It eschews simplistic gathering of facts for a complex construction of context. Ethnography properly understood can be a key method to create a shared methodology between architecture and HCI.

A unique theoretical perspective on HCI is provided by the works of Paul Dourish.[8] His early work is a historical analysis of four forms of computer interaction based on the human skills that are engaged. *Electrical interaction* creates interaction using electrical devices that are custom built of electrical components suitable for a specific narrowly defined purpose. *Symbolic interaction* emerged with the development of digital computers in the 1950s and an understanding of the capacities of the stored programs. Interaction with machines involved using assembly languages and was typically done using punch cards for both software and data. *Textural interaction* became more common as the symbolic interaction could be done directly with computers using video terminals and keyboards. Higher level programming languages with strong abstraction more easily understood by the expanding pool of users included JAVA, Basic, and C++. Textural interaction has remained important even with the introduction of more sophisticated interfaces. *Graphical user interfaces* (GUIs) included a mouse and the use of the screen as a two (or implicitly three) dimensional space and became dominant in the 1980s. GUIs engaged the use of peripheral attention, pattern recognition, spatial reasoning, visual metaphors, and information density. It was much easier for non-technical users since its logic was not based on complex mathematical understanding but rather on forms of visual thinking familiar in commonplace settings. It has remained the dominant interface for more than 30 years. Finally, Dourish proposes the opportunity for *embodied interaction* based on the user's familiarity with everyday physical and social settings. The use of computational interfaces in settings ranging from doorbells to watches to refrigerators to automobiles to thermostats to phones all have in common a central concern with the everyday world in which people live and how to integrate intelligence and interaction in a real world rather than a symbolic way.

Dourish's later work in collaboration with Genevieve Bell's[9] is an extension of the idea of embodied interaction focused on *ubiquitous computing*. An analysis of the process of design identifies the technological bias in this field and the lack of a theoretical understanding of the human setting.

In particular, the one-sided use that is made of ethnography limits the possibility of creating "thicker" connections between humans' directly experienced physical and social setting and new forms of interaction. This relationship between ethnography and design is a central concern for our book.

There is no necessity that architecture, computer science, and ethnography share a common set of assumptions and goals, but the ways in which the disciplines have developed are interestingly parallel, making possible a transformed understanding which might allow them to collaborate in a meaningful way. In this book we suggest "architecture user interface" in an attempt to address the possibilities offered by the overlaps of aspects of architecture and HCI. This is the result of an ongoing collaboration between the three authors, in architecture, computer science, and ethnography. We have through discussions, projects, and research tried to develop a clear and useful description of an architectural use interface.

The development of forms of interaction suggested by ubiquitous computing[10] and its variants has become a central research area within HCI. While it is not the only branch of research within computer science, it is certainly one of the most closely associated with contemporary concerns. This leads to an intense interest in the setting for computers, understood not as separate from their architectural setting but rather intimately connected to it. At the same time, the position of computers as distinct and iconic objects is lessened. It is sometimes hard to tell where the "computer" is at all.

Architects are more and more interested in how the computer and other digital devices can be integrated into both their practices and into the space of architecture – what we might call the methods of architecture and a transformed idea of the medium of architecture. It has become commonplace to have interactive video installations as a prominent feature of new architecture, even if little concern is paid to how they will be programmed and sustained. It is this second idea that overlaps in substantial ways with HCI. In university settings where we all three work, it is not hard to read the status of department and institute by the size of the video screen as a signal of status: currently a 40-inch screen for student services, a 70-inch screen for academic departments and institutes, a 100 inch for the provost, a full wall size for the chancellor.

It is equally true that no discipline's conceptual understanding of the role of space is very complete. HCI's understanding of the setting is often initiated by hardware and software possibilities without acknowledgment of the large role that space plays as the location for interaction. It often lacks an understanding of the mix of computational devices and ordinary space that defines ubiquitous computing settings. Architects have dealt with human occupation of space for hundreds of years, but there are significant limits to their effectiveness. At the most banal level, architectural programming, usually written as a list of spatial requirements for a building design, is specifically excluded from an architect's normal professional service. More significantly, architects have very limited knowledge of how human interaction operates in practice, an almost mirror image of the problem facing HCI.

Ethnography provides a methodology describing and analyzing culturally and socially situated practices.[11] The practice of ethnography is currently engaged in a variety of disciplines including sociology, political science, public health, and computer science. Its longest history emerges from the discipline of anthropology, in which the understanding of space has moved from the notion that a physical location shapes culture to the idea that there is instead a sense of place, created within certain spaces, by the people who inhabit them. Place is constructed from a complex interaction of everyday practices,[12] memories, and imagination, and is both connected to and distinct from physical spaces.[13] Given that the unit of analysis in anthropology is the social group, studies of public and private places focus on the social structures and cultural meanings that infuse and create places. Social structures (gender categories, economic classes, racialized differences, age categories) inform the ways that people encounter not only physical spaces, but also the people they can find and interact with within those places.[14] The development of digital places and platforms has required anthropologists to adapt their methodologies to describe and analyze human behavior taking place in virtual places, where observation requires going beyond traditional embodied field methods.

Any place, then, is produced by the presence of people in a space, or a series of spaces. Place is a cultural artifact, because it is the actions of people in a space that give meaning and definition to the place. The meanings people associate with place, sometimes captured in words such as "home" or "plaza" or "work," rise from collective and repeated individual interactions that are situated in larger cultural structures and identities.

Contemporary discussions within anthropology are also informed by the experiences of people who are immigrants, or otherwise displaced. Their attachment to and creation of place is often accompanied by a dislocation, or an inability to feel at home in places where they are forced to try to live their lives. In these cases, notions of place become even more separated from physical spaces, to the extent that some places only exist in the minds and memories of people, no longer to be found in the physical world at all. Architectural settings become places by virtue of the interactions that take place in them, and the meanings inscribed upon those spaces in the course of those interactions.

The need to understand how people perceive and create a sense of place is behind much of the current enthusiasm for ethnography in HCI. It is seen as a way to discover specific implications for design that can be readily applied. But the theoretical basis of interpretive ethnography suggests that objective criteria are less important than a grasp of the meaning which can vary widely by circumstance. It must help us to differentiate a wink from a blink, identical physical actions, when stripped of cultural context. The issue is different for architecture. Both the professional responsibilities and the structure of the resulting discourse work against serious or sustained consideration of how architecture is interpreted outside the professional community. It is seen as unproblematic.

We have already noted that ubiquitous computing has led to a proliferation of interfaces. Particular interfaces arise for particular settings. A phone is different from a laptop, different from a smart watch, different from a doorbell. Many of these interfaces are tightly connected to a specific hardware and software. The market driven focus of technology companies emphasizes a narrow and replicable understanding of an interface. But the suggestions implied by interpretive ethnography demands a more complete understanding of the web of meaning that reflects its setting. In particular, an architecture interface will need to operate using interaction that is uniquely suited to the human occupation of architecture, which we propose is the position and movement of people. It will afford specific possibilities but will need an ethnographic understanding that is in-person, open ended, and "thick."

We propose a five-part hypothesis in this book. First, that the emergence of embodied interaction has drawn architecture and HCI closer together into a shared medium. Second, both disciplines will need to adapt – HCI by widening its scope and architecture by focusing less on the intentions of the designer and more on the user. Third, that ethnography understood as both a method and a theory is critical to creating a discourse between the disciplines. Fourth, that interaction in architecture can be defined ethnographically and understood by the position and movement of people within architectural settings. Fifth, that the nature of HCI is inherently concerned with thousands or even millions of points of data extending over time frames that open unique opportunities for architecture.

The main body of this book investigates two themes, one focused on theory and one on design. While we recognize that the distinction between theory and design is not the same in all disciplines or indeed at all times, it is still vital to our contention that an understanding of the overlap in theory and design between these disciplines creates a unique opportunity for interdisciplinary collaboration that may transform both disciplines. We begin with four chapters focused on theory.

Chapter 2 is a survey of digital theory related to architecture covering the last 40 years. This begins with the work of William Mitchell starting in the 1980s, first on shape grammar[15] and then shifting with his trilogy of books[16] promoting the emergence of a digital alternative to conventional architecture. Digital methods beginning late in the 20th century spurred by Non-Uniform Rational B-Splines (NURBS) modeling and then the turn to the use of computation for fabrication led to alternative theoretical approaches. The goal is to gain an understanding of this work and relate it to those emerging in computer science.

Chapter 3 examines the emergence of HCI theory as the central concern of computer science. We trace the development of the field from a simple stimulus response model[17] to increasingly sophisticated models of psychological and human machine settings.[18] We include a discussion of ubiquitous computing, the internet of things, augmented reality, and smart building.

Chapter 4 discusses the growing interest and issues arising from the use of ethnography in HCI. It also introduces interpretive ethnography as a contemporary understanding of how meaning can be understood in specific settings. Relying primarily on the work of Clifford Geertz, we outline this development and suggest how it can be applied to both architecture and HCI. This chapter presents an example of an extended ethnographic study of a specific public setting.

Chapter 5 concerns the work of J. J. Gibson[19] that introduces the idea of ecological perception. He understands that the physical and spatial setting is fundamental to how we perceive the world. This work suggests a revised understanding of how to record and understand the geometry of the world. We propose the primary importance of position and movement as the affordances of architecture and connect it to the importance of spatial cognition as an important way of knowing the world visually. A comparison is made with the more contemporary social affordance approach of Donald Norman.

Chapter 6 deals with the central importance of movement over the long history of architecture and as an emerging factor in embodied HCI. The use of sensing technologies are discussed including radio frequency identification (RFID), Bluetooth beacons, and computer vision to understand the location and movement of people within a building. We present a wide variety of applications of this technology and an evaluative system based on sensing devices, privacy, inclusiveness, analytic techniques, and research goals. We include a system named Visual Analytics for Large Scale

Ethnography (VALSE).[20] The potential for such a system to selectively collect information about users and to be useful in understanding changes in behavior over time is discussed.

Chapter 7 concerns the integration of information into architecture and HCI. Central to this is an understanding of augmented reality (AR) as a method to combine location and meaning with the goal of creating mixed reality architectural settings. A survey of the development of AR is followed by examples of design that use AR in architectural settings. We also demonstrate how architects can design spaces with embedded AR interactions through a synthesis of 12 architects' process of designing a museum with embedded AR, as well as a brief design study of AR proxemic interactions for museums.

Chapter 8 examines site specific installations incorporating user interaction. Based on a survey of 50 examples we present a detailed analysis of 11, including work by Lars Spuybroek, Diller + Scofidio,[21] Rachel Dickey, and others at different scales and suggest criteria for judging their success. Specific attention is given to how interaction is managed, how space is integrated with interaction, and how an idea of ethnography is integrated into the work.

Chapter 9 is a conclusion and introduction to the concept of architectural user interface, a prospect for closer collaborations between architecture, HCI, and ethnography. We have demonstrated how these fields share some theoretical interests and specific analytic or design expertise in building scale settings, but need to develop new methods if interaction is to be at the core of a new collaboration. We also show how ethnographic theory and narrative can be a critical link in this effort and identify position and movement as the critical forms of interaction. Implementing these strategies offers the prospect of creating an architecture user interface, a hybrid discipline of the best ideas from both fields.

Sub-disciplines in computer science (indeed the discipline itself) are not given in advance, but rather are the result of experimentation and testing on new methods as they present themselves. Gaming, visualization, design, and creativity among many others have developed rich research agendas. Our goal is to find evidence of an emergent possibility of an architectural user interface and imagine how it can be encouraged to present a set of questions and methods that can be provocative and rewarding.

Notes

1 Wigley, Mark. *The architecture of deconstruction: Derrida's haunt.* MIT Press, 1995.
2 Jencks, Charles A. "The language of post-modern architecture." *Journal of Aesthetics and Art Criticism* 37.2 (1978).

3 See for example Lynn, Greg, and Therese Kelly. *Animate form*. Vol. 1. New York: Princeton Architectural Press, 1999.
4 See for example Carpo, Mario. *The second digital turn: Design beyond intelligence*. MIT Press, 2017, and Picon, Antoine. *The materiality of architecture*. University of Minnesota Press, 2021.
5 https://www.statista.com/statistics/610271/worldwide-personal-computers-installed-base/.
6 Grudin, Jonathan. "From tool to partner: The evolution of human-computer interaction." *Synthesis Lectures on Human-Centered Interaction* 10.1 (2017): i–183.
7 Geertz, Clifford. *Thick description: Toward an interpretive theory of culture. The interpretation of cultures: Selected essays* 3: pp. 3–30. Basic Books New York, 1973.
8 Dourish, Paul. *Where the action is*. MIT Press, 2001.
9 Dourish, Paul, and Genevieve Bell. *Divining a digital future: Mess and mythology in ubiquitous computing*. MIT Press, 2011.
10 Weiser, Mark. "The computer for the 21st century." *ACM SIGMOBILE Mobile Computing and Communications Review* 3.3 (1999): 3–11.
11 McDonald, D.W., et al., Proactive displays: Supporting awareness in fluid social environments. *ACM Transactions on Computer-Human Interaction*, 2008. **14**(4): p. 1–31.
12 Levin, D.Z. and R. Cross, The strength of weak ties you can trust: The mediating role of trust in effective knowledge transfer. *Management Science*, 2004. **50**(11): p. 1477–1490.
13 Ruef, M., Strong ties, weak ties and islands: structural and cultural predictors of organizational innovation. Industrial and Corporate Change, 2002. **11**(3): p. 427–449.
14 Gaver, W.W. The affordances of media spaces for collaboration. in *Proceedings of the 1992 ACM conference on Computer-supported cooperative work*. 1992. ACM.
15 Mitchell, William J. *The logic of architecture: Design, computation, and cognition*. Cambridge, MA: MIT press, 1990.
16 Mitchell, William J. *City of bits: Space, place, and the infobahn*. MIT Press, 1996. Mitchell, William J. *e-topia: Urban Life, Jim# But Not As We Know It*. MIT Press, 1999.
Mitchell, William J. *Me++: The cyborg self and the networked city*. MIT Press, 2004.
17 See for example Card, Stuart K., Thomas P. Moran, and Allen Newell. *The psychology of human-computer interaction*. CRC Press, 2018.
18 Hutchins, Edwin. *Cognition in the Wild*. MIT Press, 1995.
19 Gibson, James J. *The ecological approach to visual perception: Classic edition*. Psychology Press, 2014.
20 Sauda, Eric, Chris Beorkrem, Richard Souvenir, Donna Lanclos, and Scott Spurlock. Intelligent architectural settings using a computer vision based visual analytic interface. The Next City: 16th International Conference CAAD Futures 2015, pp. 175–189.
21 A good example of this work is Betsky, Aaron, et al. *Scanning: the aberrant architectures of diller+ scofidio; [on the occasion of the exhibition… at the Whitney Museum of American Art, New York, March 1–May 25, 2003]*. Abrams, 2003.

2

ARCHITECTURE

Theory and practice

Bruno Latour, a leading theoretician in the field of science and technology studies, discusses architecture in his article "Tapping lightly on Koolhaas's architecture with a blind person's cane ...,"[1] commenting on the fascination of architects (in particular Rem Koolhaas) with theory:

> Since architects, it is well known, devour a general theory at every breakfast, a philosopher who sits at their table is always in Tom Thumb's situation: for the Ogre who receives him, he is only fresh meat ... there is always a little philosophy in architecture and a great deal of architecture in philosophy.
>
> (p. 71)

Theory

In this chapter, we will begin with broad theoretical discussions of the use of computers during two periods of particular interest in architectural theory, the first in the 1990s and the second in the 2010s. While it is possible to create a more extensive bibliography of literature that conjoins computation and architecture, the majority of works are in the form of monographs with examples of architectural design and explanations of methods. In a later chapter on interactive art and architecture installations, we focus more narrowly on such individual examples.

Later in this chapter, we broadly examine the literature of digital architectural theory using advanced analytic analysis of CuminCAD, a cumulative index of research papers in computer aided architectural design

DOI: 10.4324/9781003363392-2

(CAAD), containing 12,300 records and offering us a rich collection of research data. We do not aim here to form an encyclopedic record leading to a single unified theory of architecture and human–computer interaction (HCI), but rather to investigate the ways these fields overlap and diverge, sometimes directly supporting each other and sometimes going their own ways.

Theory in architecture includes ideas and concepts shared (or perhaps borrowed or stolen) from other disciplines. We have witnessed shifting, recurring, and overlapping theories including: postmodernism, founded explicitly on historicism; phenomenology, based largely on the philosophers Heidegger, Husserl, and others; deconstruction, based on the work of the French philosopher Jacques Derrida; Sustainable architecture, or more broadly, the response to the climate crisis, based on the work of ecologists and climate scientists; social justice theory, focusing on equity issues for marginalized people; and of course, current concerns with the influence and implications of the spread of the computer. It is on this last concern that we will focus.

By the beginning of the 1990s, with the introduction of AutoCAD, computer aided design (CAD) had become widespread within architecture (driven largely by the engineering profession and large general contractors). Software originally designed for animation and film (e.g. Cinema4D, Maya) provided sophisticated tools for more complex formal exploration mostly based on Non-Uniform Rational B-Splines (NURBS) modeling. Unlike mesh modeling, which uses a network of polygons to approximate shapes, NURBS employs smooth, mathematically defined curves and surfaces. This precision resulted in the half-ironic description of "blobitecture," a style characterized by its organic, amorphous, and seemingly boneless forms.

First digital turn

An example of this first flush of enthusiasm for the digital transformations in architecture is an article by William Mitchell[2] titled "Antitectonics: The poetics of virtuality" written in 1998. It begins with a description of *Studies in Tectonic Culture*[3] by Kenneth Frampton, a study of contemporary architectural form as an evolving poetic of structure and construction with no mention at all of computers or digital ideas. Mitchell uses this as a straw dog, useful for contrasting the traditional concerns of architectural materiality with what he sees as the emerging possibilities of "virtuality." He then proceeds to draw a series of contrasts including the material/electronic; craft/computer aided design and manufacturing; local/global; facade/

interface; tectonics/electronics; ornament/electronic display; permanence/reconfigurability; and parti/genome. He concludes with the call to "retire the exhausted dogma of architectural composition and construction as our world is rewired" (p. 216).

This polemic article was written during the same period as a trilogy of immensely popular books by Mitchell, all of which outline the transformations of wireless technology and the emergence of an interconnected world. *City of Bits*[4] published in 1996 is largely focused on an expanded set of contrasts between organizations using traditional architectural concepts and new electronic organizations taking full advantage of electronic means. *E-topia*[5] in 1999 extended this discussion to include in particular full access to the web for people and devices. *ME++*[6] in 2004 arrives on the brink of the introduction of the iPhone and the explosion of the use of smartphones. Electronic connection is not just at fixed locations but is always with you.

Mitchell's work is also directly related to the enthusiasm in Silicon Valley for creative destruction as the replacement of existing organizations with electronic based models (Airbnb, Amazon, Netflix). More theoretically, the roboticist and futurist Hans Moravec's desired to "bypass all sensory processing description" and embrace "a densely connected cyberspace."[7] He imagines transplanting our fallible brain permanently into cyberspace.

In the early 2000s, there was enthusiasm for the creation of a theory of digital architecture inspired by the digital practices quickly spreading through the profession. Inspired by Mitchell's suggestion that architects drew what they could build, and built what they could draw, Kolarevic's *Architecture in the Digital Age: Design and Manufacturing*[8] is a call for information master builders, a loosely defined understanding of the possibilities for the incorporation of CAD and particularly computer aided manufacturing. This work began as an international symposium in 2003 that included self-conscious adoption of digital modeling in various forms including a complex curvilinear formal vocabulary and use of techniques including parametrics, NURBS, datascapes, and generative and performative procedures. Mass customization is introduced as an important alternative to mass production, consistent with the desire to create unique architectural forms. It includes many examples of avant-garde architectural designs as well as theoretical positions from architects and philosophers. As one might expect, the result of this heterogeneous mix of interests, expertise, and methods is not a cohesive theory, but rather a wide range of new possibilities.

"Theory and design in the first digital age"[9] by Oxman is at least a cohesive attempt to understand digital architecture design. This model places design literally at the center of a process that includes representation, generation, evaluation, and performance. Without explanation, these elements are interconnected only to design at the center or to adjacent elements. Oxman examines ways that these elements have been changed by the use of digital methods beginning with digital representation (CAD software) but expanding to automated methods of evaluation (e.g. complex fluid dynamics) and generation (e.g. artificial intelligence). While this model allows for new methods to be incorporated and interconnected into a known process, it assumes that the process will remain structurally identical. In particular, the importance of design within HCI requires a more thorough understanding of how design may evolve for both HCI and architecture.

Second digital turn

A second wave of excitement within architecture has been the focus of two leading architectural historians in the last decade. Both explicitly address the need for a more coherent theory for digital architecture.

Antoine Picon's *The Materiality of Architecture*[10] presents a wide ranging historical and theoretical explanation of a central concern of architecture. He focuses on the understanding of matter, materials, and materiality, which is central to his position: matter as the most generic description, materials as matter organized and modified by human use, and materiality as material understood in relation to human thought and practice. Picon makes a strong historical argument for the central role of materiality as the possibility for architectural expression. His explicit goal is to interpret the experimentation of the 2010s as an attempt to fuse materiality with the digital, to connect matter with humans. An impressive and often convincing array of architects and theoreticians are presented (including as a small sample LeCorbusier, Baxandall, Derrida, Deleuze, Vitruvius, LaTour, Foucault, Lynn, Tschumi, Bateson, Sullivan, Menges, Herzog, and de Meuron).

The climax of the book concerns the impact the digital will have on architecture. Blobs, parametricism, digital fabrication, "nonstandard" architecture, and discretism are identified as issues and methods that have emerged in digital avant-garde practices in the last ten years. More recently the emphasis is on emergence derived from data, on performance, and the potential for interactive architecture. Finally, he identifies two dangers: a naive return of symbolism and a reductive concern with only environmental and social concerns.

Picon is clear that these new challenges should be met in much the same way, emphasizing the necessity of materiality as a historical focus. For him, the digital ends up having been decided before it arrived.

If materiality is and has always been central, there is nothing fundamentally new, only the need to fit it into the scheme.

Mario Carpo's *The Second Digital Turn*[11] is written with careful attention to the digital methods used by "avant-garde" designers in the 2010s. He has a detailed command of the computational methods that are used by contemporary designers, and connects them to historical antecedents, for example connecting and contrasting the rise of scientific methods in the 17th and 18th centuries with current methods that rely on the ability of computer-based methods using data science. We are now in a position of having more data than ever (perhaps more than we can use). Based on the ability made common by Google search methods to store and access unimaginable amounts of data, focusing on searching that data rather than applying pre-fixed sorting categories.

Carpo makes the claim that modern science as a set of abstract principles applied to the world is made unnecessary by a new science of form searching that emerges as machines are able to generate multiple designs and evaluate and test for new potentials – form seeking through digital models using simulation. The emergence of NURBS based geometry and free form combine to allow a vastly wider set of possibilities. The possibility of expanded and even "excessive" resolution gives a new conceptualization of decoration and form. Cellular automata and hyper-realism provide new options for design. 3D scanners and 3D modeling provide technologies to directly deal with spatial design without the need for verbal or visual simplifications. Economies without scale can allow designers to use non-standard design allowing mass customization to become a reality. (More questionably, he suggests that bitcoin can be understood as part of this nonstandard approach to currency.)

Two facets of Carpo's work are important for an understanding of the relationship to the theory of HCI to which we will turn to in the next chapter. The first is the claim that architects and designers are the lead innovators in digital design and the most sophisticated users of digital mass customization, perfected if not invented by designers and architects.

The most sophisticated software used in architectural design evolved and was based on CATIA software, owned by Dassault Systèmes and licensed to Gehry Technologies. As a part of the partnership that made this possible, Tom Emmrich, a member of the senior leadership team at Dassault Systèmes, served as a representative on the Board at Gehry Technologies until 2012. His evaluation of the importance of architects in driving innovation is completely at odds with Carpo's.[12]

It is worth noting that the innovations of Gehry's Digital Project software that enabled free style design using generative parametric 3D NURBS surfaces and integration directly with the manufacturer's solid modeling software were developed as features of Computer Aided Three-dimensional Interactive Application (CATIA) beginning in 1977 before the creation of Gehry Technologies and were already widely applied in industries including defense, aerospace, and automobiles. These were critical for the design and construction of the complex 3D forms of Gehry designs, such as Guggenheim Bilbao, though the software that enabled this already existed.

The difference for architecture is that the process is very fragmented. "The age of the architect being the 'master builder', therefore 'master boss', is probably 40–50 years gone," if indeed it was ever a reality outside an Ayn Rand novel. Owners are usually focused on financial results or organizational necessities. Architects are largely focused on hourly service, and general contractors on controlling costs and schedules. Everyone in the process is risk averse. Industries that have seen the benefits of technology are concentrated and susceptible to organization. In architecture, everything is still a "one off."

The second of Carpo's claims is his discussion of the failure of the participatory turn reported in his book. He presents this as an almost inevitable result of the authorial role that architects (or at least starchitects) assume with clients. A participatory process assumes no single author, a position that will require a radical shift in the politics, power, and prestige of the profession. If anything, the development of a more extreme reliance on an avant-garde focused on originality[13] marginalizes everyone except the elite. Architects have shown no interest in opening the gates.

Finally, we should note that architects and theorists have used the very broad term "digital" to describe the field for over 30 years. While this allows the inclusion of a wide range of ideas, methods, and products, it does little to define the particularity of the research. We shall in the next chapter see the contrast with HCI (note how we begin with a subset of computer science) that continues to develop more and more defined subfields.

Practice

One aspect of the problem of "opening the gates" mentioned above is digital design and theory conducted through speculative design work, integrating computation into design and fabrication. To provide context, we present a single example; the Institute for Computational Design (ICD) ICD/Institute for Building Structures and Structural Design (ITKE) Research Pavilion of 2013–2014[14] by Professor Achim Menges of the Institute for Computational Design and Construction (ICD) at the University of Stuttgart. This project does not respond to a specific client need, but rather showcases the potential of novel design, simulation, and fabrication processes (see Figure 2.1).

FIGURE 2.1 ICD/ITKE Research Pavilion 2013–2014. © ICD_ITKE_University of Stuttgart.

The focus of the project is a parallel bottom-up design strategy for the biomimetic investigation of natural fiber composite shells and the development of novel robotic fabrication methods for fiber reinforced polymer structures. The project leads to a winding technique for modular, double layered fiber composite structures, which reduces formwork to a minimum while maintaining geometric freedom. Functional principles of natural lightweight structures were analyzed and abstracted and transferred into a modular prototype pavilion. Through the development of computational design and simulation tools, both the robotic fabrication characteristics and the abstracted biomimetic principles could be simultaneously integrated in the design process.

Glass and carbon fiber reinforced polymers allow for the fabrication of the geometrically unique, double curved modules. Two collaborating six-axis industrial robots wind fibers between two custom-made steel frame effectors held by the robots. The material, form, structure, and fabrication are defined through the winding syntax which is an integral part of the computational design tool. The effectors are adjustable to various component geometries, with only one reconfigurable tool setup for all 36 elements. The overall geometry reacts to site-specific conditions of the public space around the university building in close proximity to the park, exploring novel spatial qualities and expanding the tectonic possibilities of architecture. This work remains separate from the human and interactive foci important to HCI and ethnography, instead presenting itself as exotic.

Published research

A focused discourse on digital architectural theory and methods is represented by research papers indexed by CuminCAD, a cumulative index of CAAD. It includes bibliographic information for over 12,300 records from journals and conferences including the Association for Computer Aided Design in Architecture (ACADIA), the Arab Society for Computer Aided Architectural Design (ASCAAD), the Association for Computer-Aided Architectural Design Research in Asia (CAADRIA), Education and Research in Computer Aided Architectural Design in Europe (eCAADe), Sociedade Ibero-Americana de Gráfica Digital (SiGraDi), International Conference on Computer-Aided Architectural Design (CAAD futures), and others. These data are fully searchable.

Over time, CuminCAD conferences have covered a wide range of topics. We are interested in how these topics have evolved, and how topics are parallel to research published at HCI conferences discussed in Chapter 3. Our expectation, from experience as researchers in these areas, is that HCI conferences are much more concerned with understanding how humans think and behave, while researchers in architectural technology are more concerned with buildings, the discipline of architecture, and how technologies serve designers' choices and goals.

We use a computational approach to automatically group abstracts published at CAAD conferences using pre-trained Large Language Models to extract numerical representations of each abstract (embeddings), like points in a space. These numerical representations are useful because we can then find out which articles are closer to each other, and consecutively identify clusters of articles that are densely close to each other. In addition to numerical representations, Topic Models provide keywords that are best representative of the abstracts within that cluster. For example, a group of abstracts that cover video games might include keywords such as "controllers" and "gameplay."

After extracting topics and keywords from the collection of abstracts, we count how often each topic has appeared in each year since the conferences started. Topic modeling provides a road map of the important relationships among papers that are too numerous to analyze manually. To conduct topic modeling, we used a library in the Python programming language titled BERTopic.[15] As described by the author, "BERTopic is a topic modeling technique that leverages Huggingface transformers and c-TF-IDF to create dense clusters allowing for easily interpretable topics whilst keeping important words in the topic descriptions." Unlike other topic modeling methods such as Latent Dirichlet Allocation (LDA), the density based clustering method utilized by BERTopic can automatically determine the appropriate number of topics. However, to make the analysis and representation of topics more interpretable, we reduced the resulting smaller topics to 30, more general, topics. It is important to note that topic modeling is not an accurate representation of the diversity of topics in different papers: any extracted topic, discussed here, is probably an over-simplification of the diversity of research architectural technology and HCI (see Chapter 3). However, through the comparison of general topics covered in both disciplines we can learn about general trends that are drastically different in both disciplines.

Our central question is to understand the general interests of architects in technological advancements and if researchers in architectural technology have the same concern for human problems as those in HCI. Also, do new research traditions emerge as new societal problems emerge? We focus our attention first to conferences associated with the integration of architecture and technology, namely ACADIA, CAADRIA, eCAADe, SIGraDi, ASCAAD, and CAAD futures. To explore these questions, we can look at a topic model of abstracts from these conferences. The prevalence of CAD as a framework is due to the considerable history and wide acceptance of it in the profession of architecture as well as engineering and construction.

To visually represent the extracted topics over time, we use a stream graph. The width of each stream shows the relative frequency of a topic at a specific year. We intentionally removed counts of each year since we are more interested in how prevalent topics change in relation to other topics within the architecture discipline. The stream graph in Figure 2.2 shows the evolution of topics in CAAD conferences. The first CAAD conferences started in the early 1980s and are home to a thriving research community. We see topics emerge, ranging from virtual reality, simulation, design research, and urban planning. These are topics familiar and close to the discipline of architecture. Similar to our HCI exploration, we will break down Figure 2.2 to several trends and explore the underlying patterns.

The major topics at the birth of these CAAD conferences remain prominent to this day. Topics of architectural design, design education, and Building Information Modeling (BIM) started as the primary foci of digital architectural conferences (see Figure 2.3).

Design education is a prominent topic for the profession of architects. By far the oldest and most prominent journal associated with schools of architecture is the *Journal of Architectural Education* founded in 1947 just at the time when the idea arose of architects receiving a university degree in contrast to only an apprenticeship. The scholarship in this journal is wide ranging rather than narrowly pedagogical. It is largely theoretical and

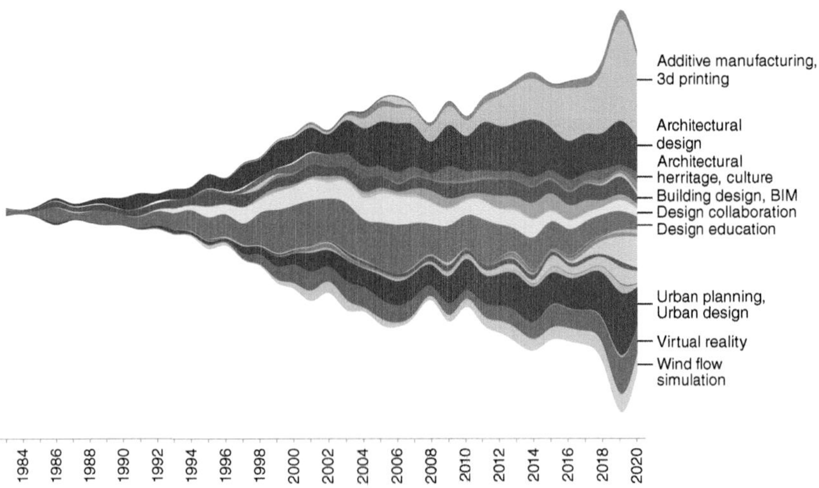

FIGURE 2.2 A stream graph highlighting evolution of all research topics extracted by our topic model within CAAD conferences.

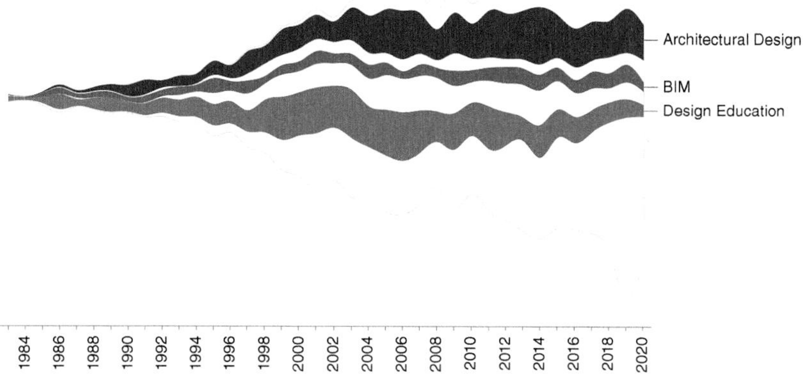

FIGURE 2.3 Topics prevalent in the early years of CAAD conferences: BIM, design education, and architectural design.

represents a justification for architecture as deserving a place in the academy. In CAAD conferences, however, the topic of design education is more specifically concerned with the pedagogy of technological concepts to architecture students. In 1990, Omer Akin published an article titled "Computational design instruction: Toward a pedagogy" that discusses the issues of teaching "design with computers."[16] As computation is a discipline, perceived to be foreign to architecture, the issue of computational pedagogy still remains important and discussed, exemplified by the paper "Teaching computational design and BIM in the age of (semi) flipped classrooms" authored by Dominik Holzer.[17]

Building Information Modeling (BIM) was another topic that gained prominence in the early years of CAAD research and still remains with a vibrant research issue. The research is concerned with creating tools for architectural design. BIM software is an example of such a tool that integrates computer modeling with architectural information. By using BIM software, architects move from dealing with points, lines, surfaces, and volumes, to architectural objects such as walls, floors, doors, and desks. For example, the paper "Representations and control of design information in an integrated CAAD environment"[18] discusses methods for effective data communication between different stages of design and streamlines the evolution of an architectural design project. The benefits of such software for architects are numerous. In common with earlier CAD software, it minimizes the time cost for drafting components of architectural spaces. More importantly, it allows for many layers of information to be integrated into the design, ranging from cost information, material and assembly properties, and information about maintenance and replacements of components and equipment.

Tracks of research that became integral in these conferences in the mid-1990s feature other disciplines and concepts important to architects (see Figure 2.4). Architectural heritage and traditional architecture are concerned with extending the well-established field of historical preservation and specifically integrating digital methods of automated scanning and computer modeling. Kent Larson's high resolution renderings of Louis Kahn's unbuilt architecture is one example of such work.[19] Another is work from Bernard Frischer on Rome Reborn, an online three-dimensional interactive model of Rome in the third century rendered in high definition.[20] CAAD research related to architectural heritage is again concerned with the challenges of computational representation and the benefits of CAAD for preserving historically important buildings. Sanchez and colleagues, in their 1997 paper titled "CAAD and historical buildings: The importance of the simulation of the historical process"[21] discuss some of the benefits of precision CAAD drawings to understand, simulate, and restore heritage buildings.

The larger stream of collaborative design is concerned with how architects can collaborate with other disciplines during the design of buildings. For example, in "Asynchronous architecture"[22] Jerzy Wojtowicz and colleagues discuss a model for collaborative design in a networked environment.

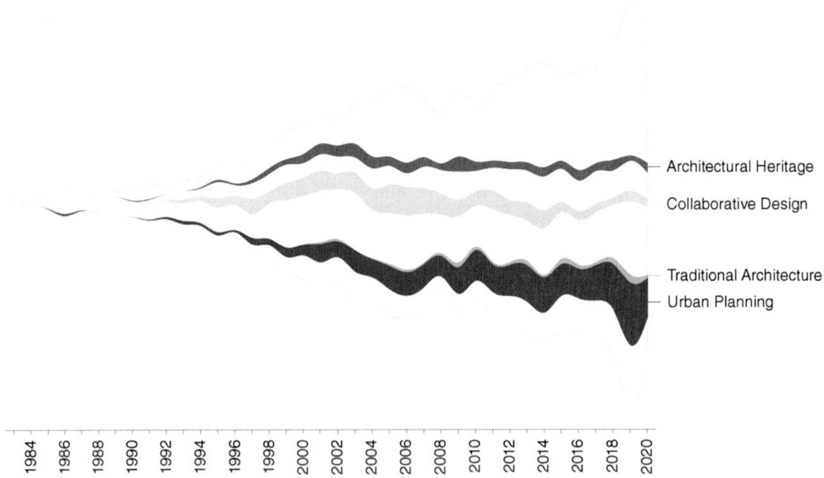

FIGURE 2.4 One emerging subset of topics in CAAD conferences in the 1990s including architectural heritage, collaborative design, traditional architecture, and urban planning.

Such approaches are in many ways an attempt to reassert the authority of architects as the leader of the design team. Problems centered on the sharing of models and knowledge between engineering, architectural, financial, and other disciplines.

Urban planning, a discipline closely related to architecture, is concerned with the study of cities, and people within cities. For architects it is often conflated with urban design; a conference by Jose Luis Sert at Harvard in 1956 where the term "urban design" was first used led to the first urban design degree in 1959. The great deal of interest in this topic indicates a sense of familiarity by architectural educators,[23] since urban design degrees are almost invariably housed in schools of architecture. In CAAD conferences, urban planning and design topics mostly revolve around development of technologies for urban planning and design processes, ranging from generating urban form[24] to simulating cities.[25]

Starting from the late 1990s and popular to this day, the major research topics at the CAAD conferences are either concerned with fabrication or simulation (see Figure 2.5). Fabrication is concerned with using computing to streamline the production of buildings. Advancements in digital fabrication and 3D printing aim to revolutionize and streamline the way buildings are conceived, designed, and constructed. These technologies allow for more complex geometry and customized elements. Discussions around these topics in these conferences revolve around new techniques, materials, and the integration of design and fabrication processes.

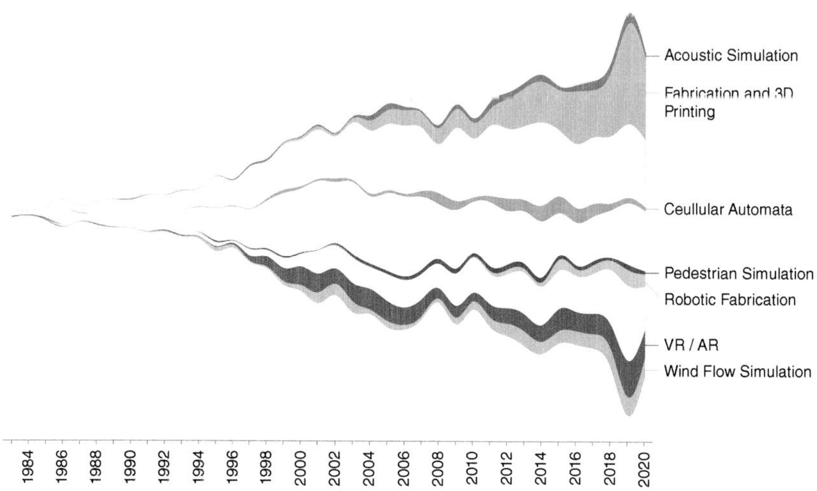

FIGURE 2.5 Subset of topics in the early 2000s covers novel technologies such as Augmented Reality (AR) and Virtual Reality (VR), simulation, and digital fabrication.

Of course, the design and implementation of buildings and spaces is a costly and time-consuming process. Simulation is concerned with helping architects understand and optimize the future of buildings and the people within them through the modeling and prediction of environmental and social processes. Often, simulation is concerned with physical aspects. Topics like acoustic simulation and wind flow simulation exemplify these trends. Simulations can also aim to model the behaviors of people within architectural spaces, exemplified by the stream around pedestrian simulation.

The late 2000s coincided with the explosive popularity of two new technologies that were seemingly unrelated to each other (see Figure 2.6). Blockchain and cryptocurrencies promised a new way of decentralized and secured transaction of data, while generative AI (GenAI) was able to generate text, images, and videos that were realistic and new. Blockchain technologies might offer radical ways to embed circular economies in buildings.[26] But it is the interest in the design and creation of new and seemingly novel building imagery that explains the explosive interests of GenAI for architects, adding to existing tools such as NURBS that can create forms that are interesting. It is with the explosive popularity and emergence of GenAI and blockchain in architecture literature that suggests that the architecture discipline, at least when it comes to how it views computing, is more concerned with how technologies can help architects design and manufacture buildings. NURBS, BIM, and GenAI helps architects efficiently bring their ideas

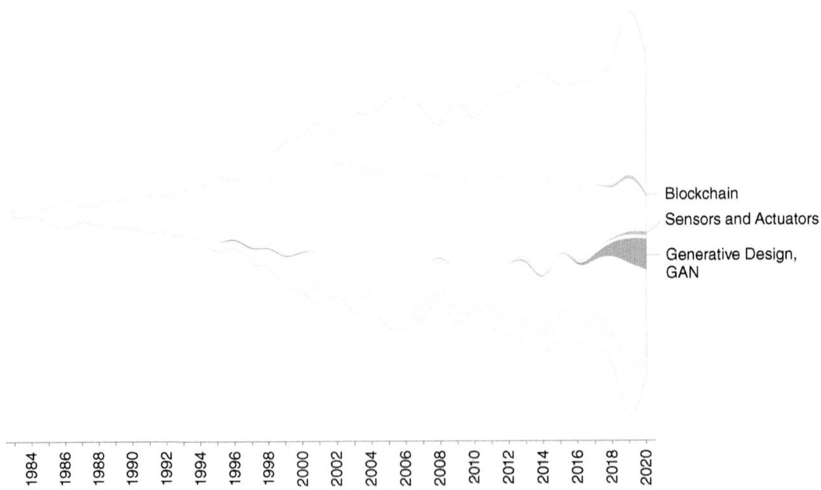

FIGURE 2.6 An emerging subset of topics in the late 2010s covers generative AI, blockchain, and sensing and actuating technologies.

to a format that can be easily turned into construction documents. Simulation allows architects to optimize spaces. Fabrications allow architects to produce them. It is very rare to see an emerging trend for architects to consider the integration of technologies in buildings, how humans behave in them, and the broader issues that might emerge from this integration.

Constraints of architectural practice

It is worth noting the particular constraints of architectural practice that limit the duration and focus of work. The vast majority of architectural practice is conducted using a shared definition of the five phases of design:

- Schematic design that creates a basic design for the shape and size of the building.
- Design development that refines and develops a more detailed set of drawings, specifications, and cost estimate.
- Construction documents including drawings and specifications submitted to local authorities.
- Bidding submittals from construction companies and their evaluation.
- Construction administration including monitoring, observing, and certifying completion.

For the United States, these definitions are created through contracts written and provided by the American Institute of Architects such as Document B100.[77] There are variations internationally, but they share a common understanding of building design, beginning with a defined need articulated by an architectural program and ending with the completion of construction. The development of the architectural program articulating the qualitative (size, number, and adjacency of spaces required) and quantitative (light, views, human activities) requirements for a building design is not a standard part of architectural design and is explicitly assumed to be the owner's responsibility. There are few data concerning what percentage of design contracts include the optional programming, but the exclusion of it from standard contracts suggests its rarity. While programming can be done within organizations or clients, the quality of the investigation can vary widely and there can be issues with how it can be effectively communicated during the design process. We will return to this again in Chapter 4 (Meaning) when the issue of the reductive use of ethnography is discussed.

Architectural design ends with the completion of the construction and with occupation of the building. The operation of the building, the human use and adaptation of the building, and the inevitable changes over time are excluded. Although post-occupancy evaluation methods have been developed, because of their expense in time and money, they are used in only a tiny percentage of buildings.

We will see in the next chapter the distinctly different design methods common in human computer interaction design that are actively engaged in the predesign understanding of the context and uses engaged during any human centered design and in the ways in which design is understood as an ongoing process of engagement with a setting. But before we leave architectural practice, we want to examine two examples of designs that extend in significant ways into what can be reasonably understood as architectural programming.

These two projects are design competitions, both of which are invited competitions aimed at attracting "starchitects" to new conceptualizations of programs that are ill defined (e.g., a national pavilion at an international exposition) or in some state of uncertainty (e.g., a library). There is the expectation that such designers will bring a strong conceptual standing to the process. And indeed both projects have important things to say and interesting and innovative ways that architecture can participate. And in the end they will illustrate the promise as well as the limits of architectural practice in a media age.

Seattle Public Library, Office of Metropolitan Architecture

The Seattle Public Library was a competition won by Rem Koolhaas and the Office of Metropolitan Architecture (OMA) and completed in 2004. OMA published a book in 2005 detailing the design, public discussion, and construction of the building.[28] It is this document that will form the basis of an analysis of the design process.

The first part of the book explains the conceptual diagrams that were part of the competition submission from OMA. Koolhaas is famous for his intention to interrogate the program; in this case he presents a set of five stable programs (HQ, book spiral, meeting, staff, and parking) and four unstable spaces between them (reading room, mixing chamber, living room, and children) where librarians inform and stimulate. The graphics for this section are very bold, non-normative presentations.

The second section primarily contains articles from the *Seattle Times* and the *Seattle Post Intelligencer* newspapers detailing meetings, presentations, letters to the editor, and construction progress updates. This section is entirely text without any graphics in an intentionally understated way. No effort is made to censor the content to eliminate criticism of the architects.

The third section is a mixture of full page photographs from the opening of the museum together with an ethnographic record with brief descriptions of the activities, and a record of what transpired over the course of the day. Interspersed with this rich set of observations is a set of normative plans, sections, and elevation.

Bruno Latour, the French philosopher and a leader of the interdisciplinary field of science, technology, and society (STS) discussed Koolhaas in his article titled "Tapping lightly on Koolhaas's architecture with a blind person's cane"[29] in *Architecture d'aujourd'jui*. He sarcastically notes architects' habit of devouring "a general theory at every breakfast," while at the same time admiring Koolhaas's embrace of contemporary ethnography. Latour's collaborator Albena Yaneva conducted just such an ethnographic study of the OMA office and Koolhaas from 2002 to 2004.[30] She extends the critique of leading architects' predilection for critical theory and the positioning of architecture in a broader and more inclusive historical and social setting as "having the ambitious task of providing a space of imaginative abstraction beyond the immediate remits and dictates of architectural practice" (p. 21). She instead gathers evidence through "voices and stories" toward reconnecting practice and meaning.

Blur/Braincoat, Diller Scofidio + Renfro

The Blur Building was a temporary pavilion built for the Swiss EXPO 2002 by the architects Diller Scofidio + Renfro. Located at the base of Lake Neuchatel in Yverdon-les-Bains, Switzerland, the structure was intended to be an "architecture of atmosphere." In a book accompanying the exposition,[31] described by the authors as "part scrapbook, part anthology of short stories," there are almost 384 dense pages of detailed discussion of the negotiations and arguments that formed the historical record over the four years of the project. The table of contents alone is challenging: love, marriage, divorce; vapor; politics of culture; white in, white out; gravityless; not a building; unspectacle; selling airwaves; reluctant icon; mounting evidence. It is an attempt to present an ethnography without an ethnographer, at least not an outside ethnographer. Every meeting, every memo, every newspaper article is presented. The implicit narrative leans heavily on the struggle of the architect against long odds to create an original design.

The Blur Building raises important questions about the nature of an architecture of nothing (but fog), about the role of media in an architectural setting and about the effect of advanced communication technology on the use of a building. It takes full advantage of the open definition of expositions to explore these issues.

Both the Blur Building and the Seattle Library present an argument for design that extends the architectural program in a way that is different from its precedents. Each presents explicit evidence of struggle and presumably triumph. They are not presented in the context of other examples, or as new prototypes that may be repeated in some form. Both designs are notable for their originality, a quality that is prized above all else in architecture.

Notes

1 Latour, B. "Tapping lightly on Koolhaas's architecture with a blind person's cane ..." *Architecture d aujourd hui* 361 (2005): 70–79.
2 Mitchell, William J. "Antitectonics: The poetics of virtuality." In *The virtual dimension: Architecture, representation and crash culture*, ed. John Beckmann: 205–17. Princeton Architectural Press, 1998.
3 Frampton, Kenneth. *Studies in tectonic culture: The poetics of construction in nineteenth and twentieth century architecture*, ed. John Cava. MIT Press, 2001.
4 Mitchell, William J. *City of bits: Space, place, and the infobahn*. MIT Press, 1996.
5 Mitchell, William J. *E-topia: Urban life, Jim – but not as we know it*. MIT Press, 1999.
6 Mitchell, William J. *Me++: The cyborg self and the networked city*. MIT Press, 2004.
7 Moravec, Hans. "The senses have no future." *The Virtual Dimension: Architecture, Representation, and Crash Culture*, ed. John Beckmann: 84–95. Princeton Architectural Press, 1998.
8 Kolarevic, Branko, ed. *Architecture in the digital age: Design and manufacturing*. Taylor & Francis, 2004.
9 Oxman, Rivka. "Theory and design in the first digital age." *Design Studies* 27, no. 3 (2006): 229–265.
10 Picon, Antoine. *The materiality of architecture*. University of Minnesota Press, 2021.
11 Carpo, Mario. *The second digital turn: Design beyond intelligence*. MIT Press, 2017.
12 Notes from meeting with Tom Emmert, February 20, 2023:

> No one runs it. The age of the architect being the "master builder", therefore "master boss", is probably 40–50 years gone. Today, no one drives the ship. The process is very fragmented. Owners are usually unsure how far to push – and certainly stay out of the messy details. A&D abandoned its lead role long ago and now is focused on hourly services, usually without the ownership of ensuring what was designed can and will be built. And the general contracting world is focused on getting it built, managing subcontractors, controlling cost and meeting schedules. This generally makes everyone in the process extremely risk averse and unwilling to try new things – and certainly unable to impose them on the other players.
>
> Relative to the operation of enterprises and industries, the real leap in technology comes when it creates two things: a single source of data and common process and tools. That means someone has to be able to impose those on the others even when the particular task that party might be doing could be harder under that system. The value is to the whole – and if no one owns the whole then no one is going to spend a lot of their own effort and risk to optimize it.
>
> It's real. Just as is the case with industrial products (cars, planes, ships), design is "easy" – making it is the hard part. ... Elon Musk discussing SpaceX and he commented something like: inventing something and making the first

one is easy. The hard part is manufacturing. Technology is used by the A&D community in their own little space, but connecting that to REAL construction and logistics is another matter.

13 Krauss, Rosalind E. *The originality of the avant-garde and other modernist myths*. MIT Press, 1986.
14 Dörstelmann, Moritz, Jan Knippers, Achim Menges, Stefana Parascho, Marshall Prado, and Tobias Schwinn. "ICD/ITKE Research Pavilion 2013–2014: Modular Coreless Filament Winding Based on Beetle Elytra." *Architectural Design* 85, no. 5 (2015): 54–59.
15 https://maartengr.github.io/BERTopic/index.html.
16 Akin, Omer. "Computational design instruction: Toward a pedagogy." *Electronic design studio: Architectural knowledge and media in the computer era*, edited by M. McCullough, W.J. Mitchell, and P. Purcell, MIT Press (1990): 301–316.
17 Holzer, Dominik. "Teaching computational design and BIM in the age of (semi) flipped classrooms." *Proceedings of the 24th CAADRIA Conference*. 2019.
18 Kim, Inhan, and Thomas Liebich. "Representations and control of design information in an integrated CAAD environment." *Computer Aided Architectural Design Future* 95 (1995): 24–26.
19 Larson, Kent, Louis I. Kahn, Vincent Joseph Scully, and William John Mitchell. "Louis I. Kahn: unbuilt masterworks." (2000).
20 Dylla, Kimberly, Bernard Frischer, Pascal Müller, Andreas Ulmer, and Simon Haegler. "Rome reborn 2.0: A case study of virtual city reconstruction using procedural modeling techniques." (2010).
Frischer, Bernard, and John Fillwalk. "A computer simulation to test the Buchner thesis: The relationship of the Ara Pacis and the meridian in the Campus Martius, Rome." In *2013 Digital Heritage International Congress (DigitalHeritage)*, vol. 1, pp. 341–345. IEEE, 2013.
21 Sanchez, Santiago, Alberto Zulueta, and Javier Barrallo. "CAAD and Historical Buildings: The Importance of the Simulation of the Historical Process." *eCAADe Conference Proceedings*, 1997.
22 Wojtowicz, Jerzy, et al. "Asynchronous architecture." *Education and Practice: The Critical Interface* (1993): 107–117.
23 De Lange, Michiel, and Martijn De Waal. "Owning the city: New media and citizen engagement in urban design." In *Urban land use*, pp. 109–130. Apple Academic Press, 2017.
24 Coates, Paul, and Miles Robin Hall. "The use of CAAD to Generate Urban Form." *CAAD Futures' 95*. 1995.
25 Borgers, Aloys W.J., I.M.E. Smeets, A.D.A.M. Kemperman, and H.J.P. Timmermans. "Simulation of micro pedestrian behaviour in shopping streets." *Progress in Design & Decision Support Systems in Architecture and Urban Planning* (2006): 101–116.
26 https://www.mdpi.com/2079-9292/8/7/724.
27 The standard form of agreement between owner and architect – AIA. Accessed August 29, 2023. https://content.aia.org/sites/default/files/2017-04/B101 2017%20sample.pdf.
28 Kubo, Michael, and Ramon Prat. "Seattle public library, OMA/LMN." (2005).
29 Latour, B. "Tapping lightly on Koolhaas's architecture with a blind person's cane…" *Architecture d aujourd hui* 361 (2005): 70–79.
30 Yaneva, Albena. *Made by the Office for Metropolitan Architecture: An ethnography of design*. 010 Publishers, 2009.
31 Diller, Elizabeth, Ricardo Scofidio, and Diana Murphy. "Blur: the making of nothing." (2002).

3

HUMAN–COMPUTER INTERACTION

Methods and theory

Donald Norman is a leading researcher and author widely regarded for his expertise in the fields of design, usability engineering, and cognitive science. His research has shaped the development of the field of cognitive systems engineering. He is primarily known for his extension of affordance theory into user experience design, especially in his book *The Design of Everyday Things*. However, more recently, he has embraced a wide understanding, beyond just "usability and usefulness," of what it means to design products and services for humans[1]:

> If beauty, pleasure, and fun are so essential to our lives, so essential to the design of products and services, then we had better come to understand these concepts. It's not enough that we build products that function, that are understandable and usable, we also need to build products that bring joy and excitement, pleasure and fun, and yes, beauty to people's lives.
>
> (p. 312)

The proliferation of computers has created a greatly expanded new audience and the need to develop new ways to engage users from a wide variety of backgrounds and abilities. In 1955, there were a total of only 250 digital computers in the world. By 2013 it was estimated that the total number of computers worldwide was 1.5 billion. One primary response to this challenge is the emergence of human–computer interaction (HCI), a large and interdisciplinary computing discipline with more than 40 years of

DOI: 10.4324/9781003363392-3

research history, concerned with the design of "human-centered" interactive technologies and interfaces. User interfaces are rapidly becoming ubiquitously embedded in almost every aspect of our world, including our buildings, and overlapping with architectural design.

During its early development as a discipline, computer science was mostly concerned with concepts like systems, algorithms, software, models, and databases. Computers were designed to make mathematical calculations fast and efficiently for expert users. It was no longer sufficient to design efficient and smart algorithms. HCI has led to a central interest in humans, users, needs, and solutions.

From optimizing human performance to acknowledging human strengths

One of the most important figures in the development of HCI is Stuart Card, a key figure at Palo Alto Research Center (PARC) and Stanford's Department of Computer Science. His career spans the period when computer science emerged as a discipline distinct from electrical engineering in the early 1970s to the present day.

In 1983, Card was the lead author of *The Psychology of Human–Computer Interaction*, a book focused on the early foundations of the field beginning in 1974.[2] The specific aim of this work is to create an empirically based cognitive theory of human performance with computers. The human mind is described as "also an information processing system" which can be described using computer software terminology. A simple model of the human mind is proposed that includes a perceptual processor, a cognitive processor, and a motor processor, each of which consists of memory and principles of operation. The author's interest is in measuring the performance of this system, including, for example, precise measures of short-term memory including capacity and decay, and cycle times measured in milliseconds. The results in this book were the basis for the first interactions with computers and eventually the foundation for graphic user interface design. The assumption was that the more like a computer we can base our understanding of the human mind, the better we can interface with it.

Fifteen years later in 1999, Card was again a lead author of a seminal book *Readings in Information Visualization: Using Vision to Think*.[3] He identifies the beginning of information visualization with the advent of the Silicon Graphics workstation in the mid-1980s which introduced advanced real-time, interactive graphics to a wide audience. He traces the advances for 15 years when these advanced features became widely available on standard PCs. This book emphasizes the use of computer-supported, interactive, visual representations of abstract data to enhance cognitive understanding. It emphasizes the complementary abilities of computer and human users. Thinking visually is a native ability for humans, but it can be very difficult for computers. By contrast, the accumulation of data is effectively unlimited for machines. Rather than trying to get humans and computers to think identically, information visualization uses interactivity and multiple data representations. It is interested in cognitive amplification through knowledge crystallization and exploration of options.

The contrast between the identical processes of humans and computers in 1983 and the open exploration and symbiosis suggested in 1999 could not be sharper. How is it possible that the same author could endorse two conceptual orders so radically different? Card starts by considering humans as an "information processing system" whose performance can be optimized. Years later, he shifts his understanding of HCI to one where humans and computers each have distinct abilities and that can collaborate.

Human-centered design

The importance of HCI in architecture goes beyond interfaces that are part of the computers in our buildings. We can also think of architecture as a potential interactive interface suited to human use. In fact, one of the most famous examples of interface design, from Don Norman's *Design of Everyday Things*, is a "door" that makes users confused. A door, along with many other architectural elements and spaces, is, in fact, a user interface. Examples are plentiful: people sit on a chair in a space, they observe the space to find their destination, and they use a handle to open a door. By learning from HCI and its evolution, we might consider architectural spaces not as static elements but as dynamic ones that adapt to the changing needs of the people who live within them.

In this chapter, we will first look at the evolutions of two very important figures in HCI research to understand how HCI researchers think about design. We will also briefly look at the evolution of many conferences that are under the umbrella of HCI.

There's probably no other book on HCI and user interface design as influential as Donald Norman's *Design of Everyday Things*.[4] The book describes how we are surrounded by designed objects that are hard and frustrating: "I push doors that are meant to be pulled, pull doors that should be pushed, and walk into doors that should be slid. Moreover, I see others having the same troubles" (p. 2). Norman brings up the door example to discuss the principle of "visibility," arguing that, for any designed object, "the correct parts must be visible, and they must convey the correct message." He also introduces other important concepts in design, such as affordance (whether an object has the ability to do something), signifiers (whether an object shows that it has the ability to do something), constraints (any limitations to what an object affords us to do), and mappings (natural and cultural analogies to make understanding a natural object). Norman introduces these concepts, along with many other important design concepts and examples, to change how objects and interfaces are designed. The idea was clear and simple: study people and design things that people can easily use without frustration.

We will return in more detail to the idea of affordance in Chapter 5 and look more specifically at the implications for architectural design. For now, we are interested in the development of HCI research.

HCI research: Modes, interactions, goals, and technologies

One of the major communities researching different aspects of HCI is the Association for Computing Machinery's (ACM) Special Interest Group in Computer-Human Interaction (SIGCHI). Beginning in 1983, SIGCHI has become home to a thriving community of research and has become the premiere conference for human factors. CHI brings together scholars from computer science, design, psychology, and social sciences. Within the conference, scholars discuss a diverse range of topics including user interface design and usability, accessibility, social media research, information visualization, human–robot interaction, games, and the ethics and impacts of computing.

Research topics in the CHI conference demonstrate an evolution that reflects changes in technology and societal needs. In the early days of CHI, influenced by the emergence of the World Wide Web and personal computers, the focus was mostly on usability and information architecture, desktop applications, and software. In the 2000s social media platforms and mobile devices sparked research in these areas. Simultaneously research on big data, AI, and novel forms of interacting with media such as augmented reality and virtual reality became prevalent within the conference. In the 2010s and 2020s, with higher awareness of the societal impacts of AI technologies, came a heightened interest in discussing how design can be beneficial to diverse populations and cultures.

Topics covered in CHI are indeed diverse and constantly evolving. However, this diversity of advancements in HCI is not confined to the CHI conference. Throughout the last 40 years, numerous special interest groups were created with more specific topical interests spanning specific interaction methods and domains.[5] For example, User Interface Software and Technology (UIST) started in 1988 with a stronger focus on engineering and technological aspects of user interfaces. Computer-Supported Cooperative Work and Social Computing focused on interdisciplinary research to support group communication and collaboration. Figure 3.1, inspired by the article "A chronology of SIGCHI conferences: 1983 to 2022,"[6] highlights this constant evolution of topics and areas of focus in CHI conferences. The dates shown are when the communities focusing on each research focus evolve into a larger, organized, special interest group (SIG) within the ACM organization. From collaborative work to play, automobiles, and sustainability, as new technologies and human and societal challenges integrate, researchers start to engage in a community of interdisciplinary research to understand and improve how humans and computers interact with technologies.

FIGURE 3.1 Evolution of SIGCHI conferences: HCI research over time.

As is evident from the name, HCI is the subset of computing research that is concerned with the design of technology in light of understanding how humans think and interact with such technologies. Over time, SIGCHI conferences have evolved to cover a wide range of topics. We are interested in how these topics have evolved, and how topics are parallel to research published at architectural technology conferences. As we explained in the previous chapter, HCI conferences are much more concerned with understanding how humans think and behave, while researchers in architectural technology are more concerned with buildings, the discipline of architecture, and how technologies serve designers' choices and goals.

To explore the parallels between HCI and architectural research, we investigated 17,000 abstracts from several major conferences including CHI, Computer Supported Collaborative Work (CSCW), User Interface Science and Technology (UIST), Special Interest Group on Graphics (SIGGRAPH) (although SIGGRAPH is not part of SIGCHI but covers related topics), and Designing Interactive Systems (DIS) to understand how these topics have evolved in response to changes in human needs. We use a computational approach to automatically group abstracts published at SIGCHI conferences using pre-trained large language models to extract numerical representations of each abstract, like points in a space. These numerical representations are useful because we can then find out which articles are closer to each other, and consecutively identify clusters of articles that are densely close to each other. In addition to numerical representations, topic models provide keywords that are best representative of the abstracts within that cluster. For example, a group of abstracts that cover video games might include keywords such as "controllers" and "gameplay."

As a reminder, we use the same method for topic modeling as discussed previously (for more detail refer to Chapter 2).

As described in Chapter 2, Figure 3.2 is a stream graph. Each stream is a topic. For example, the very bottom stream is titled visualization: it denotes abstracts that are related to the topic of data visualization. The width of each stream at each year denotes the relative frequency of abstracts in that topic for a specific year. The topics extracted from the dataset are diverse, ranging from visualization and user interface design to machine learning and healthcare. We can clearly see that a lot has happened in the 40+ years of HCI research activity. In the early 2000s, the number of research articles on HCI drastically increased. We break this chart into several ones with topics that have gained popularity around the same time. We will use these stream graphs to look at general trends in HCI research (and architectural technology later). We begin with early topics in HCI research, starting from 1974.

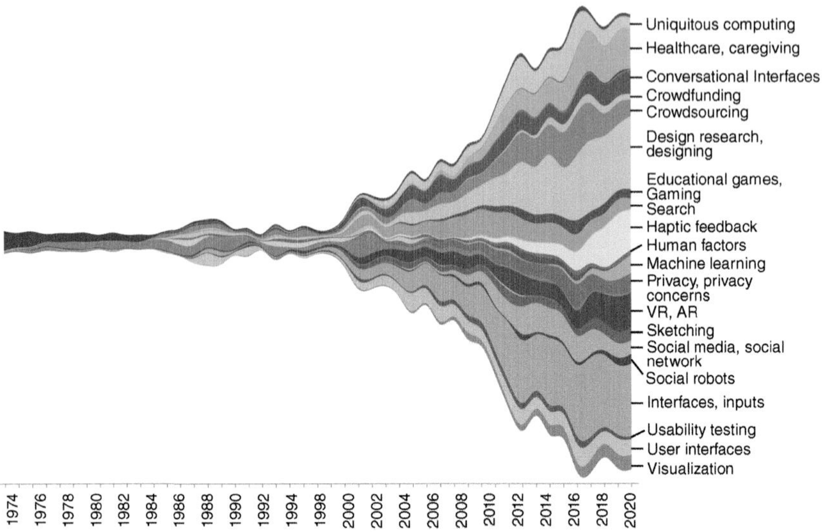

FIGURE 3.2 A stream graph highlighting the evolution of research topics in HCI conferences.

As we can see, in the starting years of HCI research, there are relatively few articles published (see Figure 3.3). In the mid to late 1970s, computers were still in the early stages and interactions were mostly done around command line interfaces. We can see the two topics around graphic interfaces and ray tracing. Let us look at some of the most cited paper titles from these topics: "Models of light reflection for computer synthesized pictures"[7] and "Casting curved shadows on curved surfaces."[8] Most of this research was published at the ACM SIGRAPH conference, which is arguably the oldest HCI adjacent research conference. Skimming through the titles and abstracts from these papers, we see that research around these topics is usually concerned with the technological challenges of creating graphic interfaces and rendering 3D and 2D information. These issues are still relevant, most of the software that architects use, such as CAD and other 3D software, are direct results of this type of research. The fact that video games, AR, and VR are currently so widely available is also directly linked to many of the advancements made in computer graphics. This might sound like a truism, but from an HCI perspective, many of the pressing technological challenges of creating graphic interfaces are at this point secondary, while understanding the needs and challenges of how humans use interfaces is more important. We can see that in the following years, new HCI topics, with more specific human-centered questions, come into play.

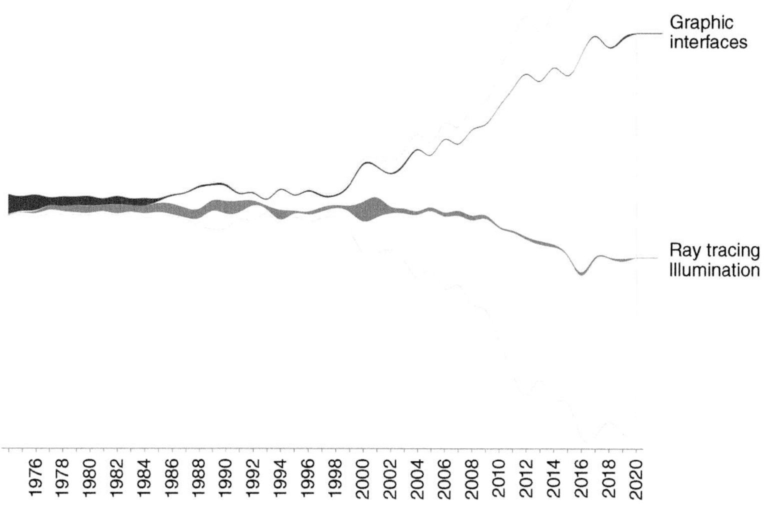

FIGURE 3.3 Early topics in HCI conferences focused on graphical user interfaces and 3D rendering techniques.

HCI research continued to influence innovation in designing novel interfaces and interactions (see Figure 3.4). The topic titled "Interfaces, inputs" includes abstracts related to input modes ranging from touch and text entry, and learning how these can be developed and improved. Conversational interfaces are similarly concerned with interactions, albeit focused mostly on conversations. In the design of such novel interfaces, however, HCI also became more concerned with the quality and usability of interfaces. A seminal paper titled "Finding usability problems through heuristic evaluation," published in 1992 by Nielsen, exemplifies this trajectory in HCI research. This work discusses heuristics or "rules of thumb" such as "visibility of system status" and "match between system and the real world" that can help designers to produce interfaces that are resilient to major problems in the usability of interfaces.[9] That was also around the time that foundational books like Norman's *Design of Everyday Things* were published.

Design research, which is one of the most prevalent topics throughout the years, is concerned with the creation of interfaces using methodologies that allow designers to directly connect with humans throughout the ideation, development, and evaluation of new interfaces. For example, "Moving out from the control room: Ethnography in system design,"[10] published in 1994 at CSCW, discusses ethnography as an important methodology for understanding the meaning behind human activities in a variety of settings.

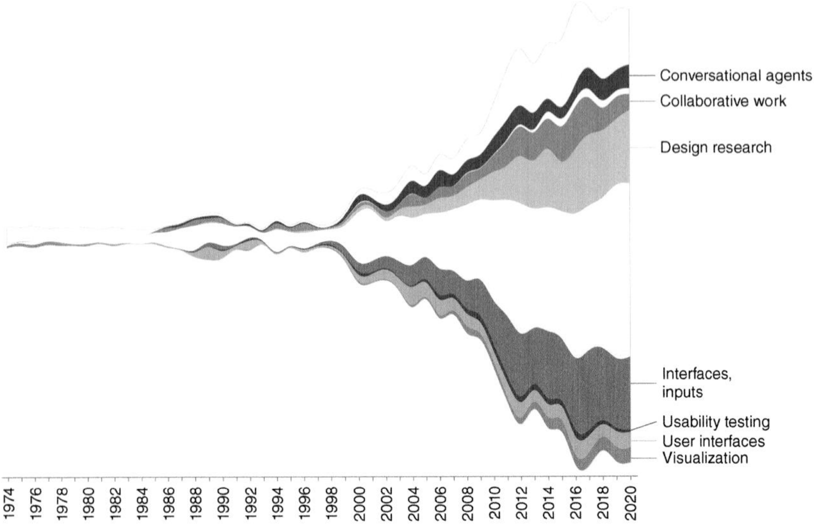

FIGURE 3.4 An emerging subset of topics in the 1990s and 2000s highlights an interest in usability studies, design research, and interface technologies.

We will go deeper into ethnography, by focusing more deeply on the works of Paul Dourish and Genevieve Bell as a methodology that can be of interest to architects, in the next chapter.

HCI research in the late 1980s and early 1990s was not solely concerned with the usability of interfaces. As computing became more powerful and integrated within different facets of human society, researchers started to focus on specific social aspects of HCI. Around that time, the prospect of collaboration through technologies started to gain attention. Computer-supported collaborative work (with a conference CSCW that emerged in the late 1980s) is an important trajectory of HCI research that focuses on understanding how people, in a variety of contexts such as organizations and work, collaborate through computer systems. Researchers in CSCW employ theories and methodologies from the social sciences in the design of collaborative work systems. For example, Malone and Crowston's "What is coordination theory and how can it help design cooperative work systems?"[11] published in 1990 discusses coordination theory or "the interdisciplinary study of coordination – that focuses, in part, on how people work together now and how they might do so differently with new information technologies."

As technological possibilities, afforded new modes of interaction in the 2000s, become advanced enough for new technologies to be used by people, so research into how humans understand, use, and integrate those interfaces into their daily lives becomes possible (see Figure 3.5).

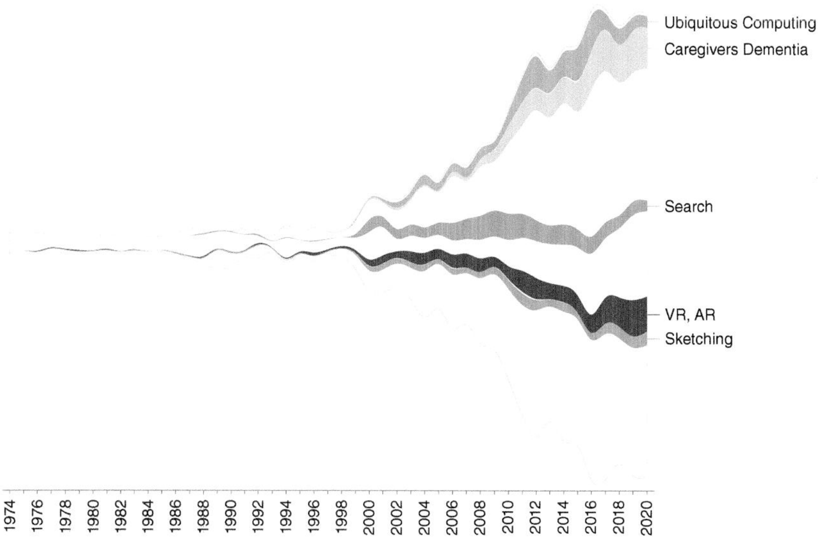

FIGURE 3.5 Emergence of ubiquitous computing and important social domains such as healthcare and internet searching in HCI research.

Virtual and augmented reality are among those technologies. Just like other types of interfaces, HCI researchers focused on designing novel interaction modes and information presentation techniques for 3D virtual environments. For example, in 2003, Garau and colleagues studied "The impact of avatar realism and eye gaze control on perceived quality of communication in a shared immersive virtual environment"[12] through an experimental study to compare basic versus photorealistic avatars.

HCI research in VR and AR goes beyond interaction modality and interface design. In the early 2010s, when VR started to evolve rapidly, HCI researchers started to consider VR issues within realms that require collaboration, such as work, education, healthcare, engineering, gaming, entertainment, and social communication. For example, "Effects of head-mounted and scene-oriented video systems on remote collaboration on physical tasks,"[13] authored by Fussell and colleagues, discusses the impact of a shared view of the work environment for remote collaboration on physical tasks.

Aside from novel technologies, HCI is also constantly concerned with technologies that are integrated into our daily lives. Considering searching as an example, there is no debate that with the dominance of Google as a search engine and the mass availability of smartphones, we rely on searching for information in almost every aspect of our lives. Moreover, searching is integrated into virtually every application. Today with the popularity of conversational AI interfaces, we are striving to perfect searching using natural language and conversation. This massive ubiquitous availability of searching is also present in HCI as researchers, starting with the popularity of search engines in the 2000s, start researching the human aspects of searching.

The study of how technologies are integrated into human life falls under ubiquitous computing (Ubicomp) which developed a strong research community and conference with the same name starting in 2001. It focuses on the proliferation of interconnected computing devices that often do not necessarily require direct user interaction. One example of UbiComp research focuses on how designers strive to gain a deeper understanding of the context of the activity. For example, Gloria Mark and colleagues, in "The cost of interrupted work: More speed and stress,"[14] measure the disruption costs of interruptions such as "the additional time to reorient back to an interrupted task" if a difference in context (e.g. person is working on a paper but is interrupted with a question about budget) has a negative effect on getting back to the task at hand.

The paradigm shift of HCI research and Ubicomp is exemplified by some of the newest trends in HCI research. In the mid to late 2000s, social media platforms became an integral part of society influencing how humans engage in activism, arts, entertainment, and commerce. Research on understanding social media became a central concern of HCI research. Studies

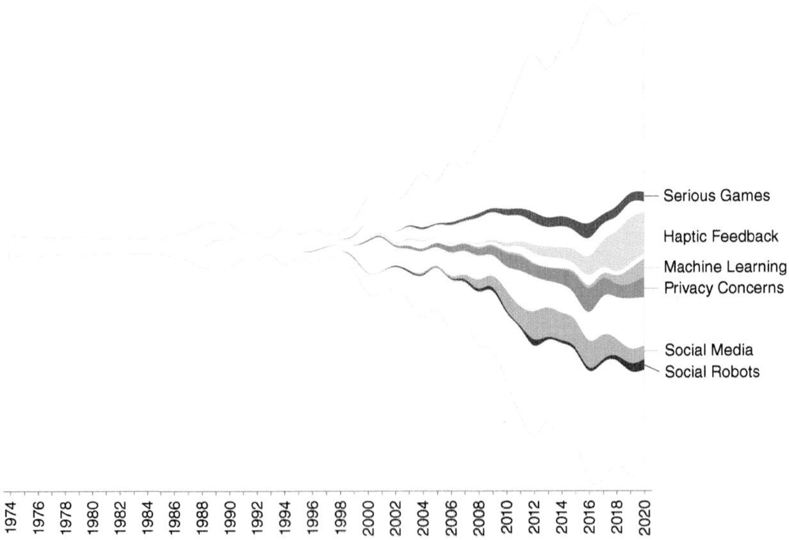

FIGURE 3.6 Other emerging topics in HCI research in the 2000s continue to respond to emerging social spaces and challenges.

on social media are numerous and diverse, ranging from the use of Twitter during natural hazards,[15] collaborations on Wikipedia,[16] and knowledge sharing in social Q&A sites.[17] With this paradigm shift, CSCW, one of the conferences that was focused on collaborative work, started to be concerned with "social computing" as well. This was due to a realization that issues of computation and collaboration were not just applicable to formal work environments but also to broader social interactions emerging on social media platforms.

In addition to new virtual spaces for humans to exchange information, social media also generated new challenges. The privacy and ethics of big data and social media were among the most pressing issues of our time, leading to several high-profile interactions between technology companies and governmental agencies in the USA and Europe.[18] A large amount of HCI research emerged around the question of designing new techniques to ensure data privacy. For example, in "You've been warned: An empirical study of the effectiveness of web browser phishing warnings,"[19] Egelman and colleagues study whether active phishing warnings impact resiliency to such attacks.

Even though addressing privacy concerns became an essential stream in HCI research, broader interdisciplinary research communities also emerged focusing on the study of such challenges. The ACM Conference on Fairness, Accountability, and Transparency (FAccT), which started in 2018, is the primary community for research around such issues.

From computer graphics, to virtual reality, to ethics and privacy in social networks, HCI research shows an active interest in responding to new conditions in human societies. As new challenges surface at the intersection of technologies and society, researchers employ a variety of methodologies to address the challenges. Architecture, a discipline focused on the creation of spaces for human activity, is also deeply interested in technologies. But, as we saw in the previous chapter, the vast majority of the interest emphasizes technologies for design, simulation, and manufacturing of buildings over an ethnographic or human understanding of the engagement with architecture. Research in HCI and architecture is working on different problems. This difference in approach, which is reflective of the practical constraints of architecture, is a core focus of this book. If technologies are to be embedded, and integrated with architecture, architects might need to think like HCI researchers.

HCI in practice: What do HCI designers do?

Many design disciplines focus on the design of a specific set of "things." For example, architects focus on designing spaces and buildings of different kinds. In doing so, they apply their expertise and knowledge about spatial organization, facade design, and architectural objects. There are numerous other design disciplines with names communicating the domain in which practitioners engage. Graphic designers design visual screens. Interior designers design interior spaces. Industrial designers design manufactured products. Practitioners of HCI take different titles when they start their practice. Human-centered design and user experience design are among the titles given to "HCI practitioners." But, what do human-centered designers and user experience designers do?

Graduate courses taught to HCI students might be a good starting proxy for understanding the details of what a human-centered designer does. As an example, the Stanford "Introduction to Human–Computer Interaction Design" course[20] starts by discussing the needs of users through various strategies such as participant observation and interviews. The course moves on to discuss the notion of user-centered design, its goals and objectives, and how creating prototypes of different fidelities and bringing the prototypes to potential users serves as an integral part of working with humans to design something. Topics of heuristic evaluation (i.e. Nielsen's heuristics) and input modalities are also covered. After going through some graphic design concepts that would be the cornerstone of the design of an interface, the course concludes by discussing methodologies for evaluating designs through qualitative and quantitative user studies.

Most of these methodologies taught in such courses are often practiced in human-centered design practice. One such practice is a prominent design agency that employs these methodologies. David Kelly, a co-founder of IDEO focusing on human-centered design, discusses their process:

> The point is that we're not actually experts at any given area. We're experts on the process of how you design stuff. So we don't care if you give us a toothbrush, a toothpaste tube, a tractor, a space shuttle, a chair, it's all the same for us. We want to figure out how to innovate, by using our process and applying it.

To design the shopping cart, IDEO designers first started by engaging in an ethnographic observation of a shopping environment. Designers observed how people interact with their carts to learn about the problems they encountered and how they solved them. They also interviewed shoppers and employees to gain a deeper knowledge about their needs. Through these observations and interviews, they found that shopping carts, as simple as they are, come with a lot of challenges. For example, they observed that some families need to not only place the stuff they buy in a cart, but also their young children! They also observed that in some store isles, space is tight and turning is difficult, so people would lift the cart to move in other directions.

Given these observations, a team of designers who come from different disciplines, would then gather and brainstorm ideas for different solutions that could potentially address the observations. They first would sketch their ideas, and then build simple, low-cost prototypes for their ideas. One of the prototypes is a modular cart in which you can place different baskets with child safety in mind. The other is designed with wheels that can be turned 90 degrees to move in tight isles.

IDEO designers would take these prototypes back to users and iterate and test with them. They might learn that some of these ideas pose new challenges and problems, some are not feasible to build financially. Through these iterations, ideas for a new product that would align more closely would come to light. The final prototype included modularity, movability, and safety as its primary needs.

The human-centered design process treats design as a means to solve specific problems for humans. Instead of focusing on specific expertise, it puts humans at the center and spends time learning about the users' needs by employing research methods such as participant observation, co-design, think-aloud, surveys, and storyboards. Numerous prototypes are designed and tested; a final design would emerge from an iterative process of prototyping, testing with users, learning, and innovating.

Interestingly, the story we told through the topic modeling of HCI research, revealed several trends that match with topics taught in the Stanford HCI course and IDEO's practice. They also show a wide topical net that aims to address facets of society which are highly integrated with technologies.

Architecture and human-centered design

In the previous chapter, we discussed the nature and constraints of architectural practice, specifically the lack of careful or extended studies of human behavior, before the building design, and a corresponding paucity of study after the building is occupied, as well as the emphasis on originality as the *sine qua non* for the field. Our exploration of CAAD research reflects a similar trend where technology research is seen as a means of enabling architects. Understanding people is predominantly done in an abstract way. People are represented by a tidy list of spatial needs (one reception area of 200 square feet, a conference room of 300 square feet, three private offices of 100 square feet each, etc.). When an attempt is made to understand more qualitatively the expectations and needs of the users, architects have no common methods within the discipline to rely on; the best representations they can muster are often plans or sections with human figures as decorative motifs. In rare cases, understanding people is abstracted to simulations of human behavior, like pedestrian movement.

The amount of detail devoted to the architect's expectations of how people might behave in a place varies a great deal. At one extreme, hundreds of thousands of office spaces and apartments can be done with almost no attention to the ultimate users. The key questions during schematic design might be how many apartment units can I put on the site? How much parking will I need? How much rent can be charged for what amenities? On the other hand, the brief for a restaurant is full of fine-grained information about human interaction. How do the waiters dress? What is the graphic language? What language should be used? For example, "You would like the Canard a l'orange, Madame. Perfect!" Two million square feet of a new edge city can be guided on the back of an envelope; one restaurant may require a novel.

Architectural programs that include multiple iterations can potentially develop a better understanding of the people who will use them. Healthcare buildings, particularly those associated with large systems, often use each new building as an opportunity to understand how, for example, outpatient surgery centers work and to refine them over time. This can lead to improvements, for example for the surgical team to identify efficiency problems with an existing design that can be improved incrementally. Similar claims are possible for school design, and retail and apartment buildings. The range of feedback from each design is critical if the feedback is to include a wider range of human response to a setting. There is a strong temptation to use simple measures to each situation: What arrangement for a grocery store generates the highest sales per square foot? What school is the easiest to control from interior and exterior threats? What arrangement of the surgical suite makes an operation take less time? There is the need for a more balanced understanding of a wide range of experiences by customers or patients, staff, and the subjective difference between open heart surgery and food and sustenance at a grocery store. The prominence that we believe ethnography needs to play in architectural design is for exactly this reason; it can provide a more complete and nuanced understanding of human behavior that prevents a single, reductive understanding.

Post-occupancy evaluation is another possibility for understanding human behavior, but that rarely influences design. This is a specific technique used to study a problem over a short period of time. Post-occupancy evaluation in surgical units, for example, seeks to understand if staff are moving efficiently. A nurse or ethnographer is sent to a site to observe. But the length of time for observation is limited by cost, and that's not a part of the standard services for an architect.

A good example of this oversimplification is the lobby of the College of Arts + Architecture building in which we have often worked. About ten years ago, a renovation of this space and the adjoining offices was completed to upgrade the image of the institution. An important part of this renovation was the installation of an updated video screen in the lobby. It was a video wall composed of four screens with a very elegant and expensive frame of steel channels. On this display, video clips of important events and interviews ran in a long loop. A very generous budget was allocated for the screens but no funding was included to create media fit for the lobby. As a result, the displays changed infrequently, the sound level was never at the right level (too soft when there was a crowd in the space, too loud when there were only a few people), and the system was completely unaware of who might be in the space, what they might be doing, and how the system might adjust. The display signaled the importance of the main office but communicated nothing.

Some possibilities for adaptation of design techniques such as storyboarding, behavior mapping, and day-in-the-life from human centered design may be possible, although the contractual limits on programming during typical architectural services make this difficult. It is even more difficult to create a possibility for understanding the ongoing use of a building over time. We will discuss one possibility for this in Chapter 8: Visual Analytics for Large Scale Ethnography (VALSE) is a system that can gather information about human use of a building over a virtually unlimited time frame.

Theoretical HCI

For computer science, what is called theory is often based on methods and processes applied to a wide set of cases. For example, computer set theory or graph theory describe mathematical procedures that can usefully be applied to computational problems. And computer ontology is not what it might imply in philosophy, a branch of metaphysics dealing with the nature of being. Instead, it is an automated set of procedures designed to extract the concepts within a subject from data, describing their properties and relationships.

A unique effort to reframe the theoretical framework for HCI is *Where the Action Is*[21] by Paul Dourish. He came to this work as a fellow at the Palo Alto Research Center focusing on tangible and social computing research.

But his interest in this book is foundational, seeking to understand the philosophical basis for the changes in computer science, specifically HCI.

As a key part of this effort, he analyzes a history of interaction models. He begins by discussing electrical interactions which essentially mean computing through the use of customized electrical circuits. He then moves on to symbolic interaction using numerical symbols and mathematical formulas and then to textual interactions using programming languages for command line interaction with computers. He then discusses graphical interfaces, which replace 1D streams with 2D interactions that use visual metaphors to afford pattern recognition and spatial reasoning which are the ones we are most familiar with through our usage of contemporary personal and mobile computers using window-based interfaces. And he finally discusses the move towards embodied interaction that involves social settings and ubiquitous computing invisibly everywhere in our lives.

The basis for his understanding of embodied interaction is based on the branch of philosophy named phenomenology. His analysis of phenomenology and its call for "being-in-the-world" leads to the need for an expanded understanding of embodied interaction. The contrasts between previous abstract symbolic systems with those required by embodied interaction leads to his emphasis on the relationship of action and meaning. His goal is to return to design and analysis with a new insightful perspective.

The focus in this chapter is not on theory per se as much as on a series of insights gathered and applied from a wide range of methods. It is certainly not true that computer science is without theory, but it is fair to say that theory often arises from the implication of the emerging discipline, rather than as a separate or primary study. In the social sciences this has been referred to as grounded theory,[22] the construction of theories through the collection and analysis of data. Inductive reasoning features prominently in guiding the coding of data or cases.

But it is also true that it would be unfair to not recognize the theoretical insights of proto-computer scientists (for the discipline had not yet been named or separated from electrical engineering): von Neumann's model[23] of the "architecture" of a digital computer (processor, control unit, memory, mass storage, input/output devices), Herbert Simon's "Cognitive science: The newest science of the artificial"[24] that extends scientific methods from nature to design, and Alan Turing's early work in artificial intelligence[25] were *ex novo* contributions to the early emergence of a conceptual framework for computer science. We will turn in the next chapter to how the emphasis on meaning is central to architectural and HCI settings.

Notes

1 Norman, Donald A. "Introduction to this special section on beauty, goodness, and usability." *Human–Computer Interaction* 19, no. 4 (2004): 311–318.
2 Card, Stuart, Moran, Thomas, and Newell, Allen. *The psychology of human-computer interaction*. Lawrence Erlbaum, 1983.
3 Card, Stuart, Mackinlay, Jock, and Scheiderman, Ben. *Readings in information visualization: Using vision to think*. Morgan Kaufmann, 1999.
4 Norman, Don. *The design of everyday things*: Revised and expanded edition. Basic books, 2013.
5 https://dl.acm.org/doi/fullHtml/10.1145/3568732.
6 Kumar, Neha, Julie A. Adams, Bill Buxton, Linda Candy, Pablo Cesar, Leigh Clark, Benjamin R. Cowan et al. "A chronology of SIGCHI conferences: 1983 to 2022." *Interactions* 29, no. 6 (2022): 34–41.
7 Blinn, James F. "Models of light reflection for computer synthesized pictures." *Proceedings of the 4th annual conference on Computer graphics and interactive techniques*, 1977.
8 Williams, Lance. "Casting curved shadows on curved surfaces." *Proceedings of the 5th annual conference on Computer graphics and interactive techniques*, 1978.
9 Nielsen, Jakob. "Finding usability problems through heuristic evaluation." *Proceedings of the SIGCHI conference on Human factors in computing systems*, 1992.
10 Hughes, John, Val King, Tom Rodden, and Hans Andersen. "Moving out from the control room: ethnography in system design." In Proceedings of the 1994 ACM conference on Computer supported cooperative work, pp. 429–439. 1994.
11 Malone, T.W., & Crowston, K. (1990, September). What is coordination theory and how can it help design cooperative work systems?. In *Proceedings of the 1990 ACM conference on Computer-supported cooperative work* (pp. 357–370).
12 Garau, Maia, Mel Slater, Vinoba Vinayagamoorthy, Andrea Brogni, Anthony Steed, and M. Angela Sasse. "The impact of avatar realism and eye gaze control on perceived quality of communication in a shared immersive virtual environment." In *Proceedings of the SIGCHI conference on Human factors in computing systems*, pp. 529–536. 2003.
13 Fussell, Susan R., Leslie D. Setlock, and Robert E. Kraut. "Effects of head-mounted and scene-oriented video systems on remote collaboration on physical tasks." In *Proceedings of the SIGCHI conference on Human factors in computing systems*, pp. 513–520. 2003.
14 Mark, Gloria, Daniela Gudith, and Ulrich Klocke. "The cost of interrupted work: More speed and stress." *Proceedings of the SIGCHI conference on Human Factors in Computing Systems*, 2008.
15 Vieweg, Sarah, et al. "Microblogging during two natural hazards events: What twitter may contribute to situational awareness." *Proceedings of the SIGCHI conference on human factors in computing systems*, 2010.
16 Kittur, Aniket, et al. "He says, she says: Conflict and coordination in Wikipedia." *Proceedings of the SIGCHI conference on Human factors in computing systems*, 2007.
17 Vasilescu, Bogdan, et al. "How social Q&A sites are changing knowledge sharing in open source software communities." *Proceedings of the 17th ACM conference on Computer supported cooperative work & social computing*, 2014.

18 For example refer to Mark Zuckerberg appearing at US congress: Alaimo, Kara. "Mark Zuckerberg Misled Congress about Privacy." CNN. Last modified December 21, 2018. https://www.cnn.com/2018/12/21/opinions/mark-zuckerberg-misled-congress-privacy-nyt-alaimo/index.html.
19 Egelman, Serge, Lorrie Faith Cranor, and Jason Hong. "You've been warned: An empirical study of the effectiveness of web browser phishing warnings." *Proceedings of the SIGCHI conference on human factors in computing systems*, 2008.
20 http://openclassroom.stanford.edu/MainFolder/CoursePage.php?course=HCI.
21 Dourish, Paul. *Where the action is: The foundations of embodied interaction*. MIT Press, 2001.
22 Glaser, B., and A. Strauss, *The discovery of grounded theory: Strategies for qualitative research*. Aldine, 1967.
23 Godfrey, Michael D., and David F. Hendry. "The computer as von Neumann planned it." *IEEE Annals of the History of Computing* 15, no. 1 (1993): 11–21.
24 Simon, Herbert A. "Cognitive science: The newest science of the artificial." *Cognitive Science* 4, no. 1 (1980): 33–46.
25 Turing, Alan M. "Can digital computers think." The Turing test: Verbal behavior as the hallmark of Intelligence (1951): 111–116.

4

MEANING

Interpretation and ethnography

The anthropologist Clifford Geertz, in his article "Thick description: Toward an interpretive theory of culture"[1] provides an overview of an interpretive theory and its role in human–computer interaction (HCI) and architecture:

> The concept of culture I espouse … is essentially a semiotic one. Believing, with Max Weber, that man is an animal suspended in webs of significance he himself has spun, I take culture to be those webs, and the analysis of it to be therefore not an experimental science in search of law but an interpretive one in search of meaning. It is explication I am after, construing social expressions on their surface enigmatical.
>
> (p. 5)

From HCI theory

An example of the use of such a theory and at the same time a counter-example to the secondary status of theory in computer science is the work of Paul Dourish. He has published research over the last 20 years that connects ongoing issues in human computing interface design with broad theoretical structures.

We discussed Dourish's first book *Where the Action Is* in the previous chapter that connects the philosophy of phenomenology with his ongoing work at Palo Alto Research Center on tangible and social computing. He discusses the emergence of four distinct interfaces since the emergence of computers: electrical, symbolic, textural, and graphical. He then carefully

DOI: 10.4324/9781003363392-4

analyzes phenomenology and how its call for "being-in-the-world" leads to the need for a new form of interface, which he calls embodied interaction.

Dourish's next work is particularly at home in the present chapter which is focused on meaning. Together with the anthropologist Genevieve Bell, in the book *Divining a Digital Future: Mess and Methodology*[2], the authors' focus is on ubiquitous computing, a concept that emerged from Xerox PARC in the 1980s under the leadership of Mark Weiser.[3] Given a backdrop of increasing availability of computing power and decreasing costs, he argues for the idea that computers should "disappear into everyday life." At first he imagined three scales of digital devices – inch size tabs, foot size pads, and yard size display – all interconnected and sharing data (a concept which roughly, but not exactly, foretells the emergence of smartphones, tablets, and wall displays). Later work expands the number of devices exponentially to include automobiles, coffee makers, alarm clocks, refrigerators, and thermostats. Weiser describes this new environment as embodied virtuality. It is obvious from Dourish's earlier work that he would be interested in this extension of the interface out from the confines of the personal computer.

As Bell and Dourish note, ubiquitous computing was unusual as a computer science research field because it is not primarily defined by a technical problem but is instead focused on a vision for real-time, real-world environments. Even at this schematic level, it is worth noting a similarity to architecture as a design field. First, as Terry Winograd, Director of the Stanford Human–Computer Interaction Group,[4] put it: "When an architect designs … a structure is being specified. More significantly the patterns of life for its inhabitants are being shaped" (p. 3). Second, the positioning of computational devices for both ubiquitous computing and emerging computational architectural settings are assumed to be situated within a spatial setting and to require an understanding of that setting. And finally, there is the necessity for sophisticated and universal connectivity if any technology is to be more than furnishings. With the emergence of Wi-Fi, Bluetooth, cellular, and other technologies, this has become widely (but still not universally) present.

From its announcement in 1991, ubiquitous computing has been aligned with ethnography. One reason is simply that the stated intention to deal with the real world makes the research methods suitable for isolated laboratories irrelevant. Ethnography has always been conducted in real-world settings and can be seen as a natural ally.

Dourish and Bell document the reliance on ethnography to produce empirical data in the form of implications for design; for example a possible design should fit in the hand, be smooth to the touch, and be silent until issuing warnings. They argue forcibly for the role of ethnography as interpretive rather than merely a list of observations. In this section we discuss an analytic ethnographic approach that provides a theory and interpretive strategies aimed at a conceptual understanding that can be used to frame the intersection of the technological and the everyday world.

In his most recent book *The Stuff of Bits*[5] Dourish is interested in the idea of materiality and the digital. We have already seen that for architects materiality is pursued in much the same way it always has been (How do we process materiality in interesting or unique ways?) using computers as sophisticated mechanisms to form material in new ways. Dourish sees a more central way in which information itself is inherently bound up in the material. He points out as example NoSQL databases without fixed categories, internet events as structured social space, and the material implications of internet routing.

Applied ethnography

Ethnography is derived from the Greek *ethnos*, meaning a cultural group; "graphy" meaning writing. It is an interpretation of the flow of social discourse, captured in a written document that can be consulted and reused. Ethnographic meaning is local, not abstract, and it is legible to others.

The anthropological understanding of space has moved from the colonial notion that a physical location shapes culture and to the notion that there is instead a *sense of place*, created by people inhabiting and revisiting certain spaces over time. Place is constructed from a complex interaction of everyday practices,[6] memories, and imagination, and is overlain on and related to physical spaces, but also distinct from a geometric description.[7] Particularly prominent in anthropological studies are concerns about social structures that infuse and create public spaces. These social structures inform the ways that people encounter not only physical spaces, but also the people they find and interact with within those places.[8] Anthropologists routinely address the fact that human behavior is not only taking place in physical spaces, but virtual ones as well, where observation requires going beyond traditional social science field methods. In *Coming of Age in Second Life*[9] Boellstorff becomes an avatar in the game and adapts surveys, focus groups, and interviews in a two year study of gender, race, sex, money, place and time, and self and group identity.

Place, then, is produced by the dwelling of people in space. Place is an artifact, a processual entity generated by the occupation, interpretation, imagination, and memory of people associated with/living within the space. The interaction of people with space gives meaning to place. A sense of place cannot exist in the absence of people; for example, *home* is a specific kind of place. The meanings people associate with place arise from individual interactions that are situated in larger cultural structures and identities.

Contemporary discussions within anthropology are also informed by the experiences of people who are immigrants, or otherwise culturally or spatially displaced. Their attachment to and creation of place is often accompanied by a dislocation, or an inability to feel at home in places where they are forced to try to live their lives. In these cases, notions of place become even more separated from physical spaces, to the extent that some places only exist in the minds and memories of people, no longer to be found in the physical world at all.

Particularly prominent in anthropological eyes are concerns about the social structures that infuse and create public spaces, and so inform the ways that people encounter not just the physical spaces that underlie the place, but also the people they find and interact with within those places.

Interpretive anthropology

Ethnography provides a methodology foreseeing culturally and socially situated practices.[10] Architectural settings become places by virtue of the interactions that take place in them, and the meanings inscribed upon those spaces in the course of those interactions.

To understand the nature of such an interpretive ethnography, we will need to look more closely at the work of Clifford Geertz, who is a central figure in its development in the last quarter of the twentieth century. He announces his interest in the semiotics of humans "suspended in webs of significance he himself has spun" (p. 5).[11] using the metaphor of thick description borrowed from Ryie. Using an analysis of the difference between a twitch and a wink, he demonstrates that the context of the setting allows one to understand their meaning; a wink requires someone ready to see its intent. It's this thick description that he claims is the proper study of ethnography, rather than this listing of facts. The goal is a stratified hierarchy of meaningful structures of signs; in this case, twitches, winks, fake winks, parodies, and so on. Geertz is particularly interested in how ethnographers can uncover such meaningful context. Rejecting an idealized or innate idea of empathy, he instead proposes understanding culture from both experience-near and experience-far perspectives (emic versus etic, inside versus outside).[12] An experience-near concept is one which an individual unselfconsciously uses to describe what he or she sees, feels, or thinks. An experience-distant concept is one that specialists (ethnographer, priest, or ideologist) employ for scientific, philosophical, or practical aims usually in multiple settings. "Love," Geertz explains, is an experience-near concept; an "object cathexis" is an experience-distant one. Ethnography needs both to escape imprisonment in either experience-near understandings only and that are entangled in immediacy, or in experience-far understandings that are subject to abstraction and jargon. Dilthey's concept of the hermeneutic circle[13] is central to how any form of interpretations actually operate, including diverse examples such as baseball and Spitzer's[14] textural explanation of Keats "Ode to a Grecian Urn." Understanding inner lives has more in common with getting a joke than receiving a sacrament.

Geertz sees the interpretive impulse operating across many disciplines;[15] citing as examples philosophy as literary criticism, scientific discussions as belle-lettres, parables as ethnography, history with equations and tables, and theory as travelog. The analogues that previously were based on craft and industry (e.g. metallurgy as mining theorized) are now often based on cultural performance. Based on ethnographic studies of which he has deep knowledge from field research in three diverse settings (Java, Bali, and Morocco) Geertz identifies a distinct sense of person unique to each. Without repeating his findings in detail, they all lead to an understanding of a culture based on oscillation between the exotic minutiae of these definitions of a person and more sweeping and abstract characterizations.

Indeed, the writing of ethnography is the subject of an advanced seminar at the School of American Research in Santa Fe with ten participants, eight with backgrounds in anthropology and one in literary studies and one in history. The resulting essays were published as *Writing Culture* in 1988. The context of this work was the growing popularity of literary approaches in human sciences, a turn from a fact based, ostensibly scientific approach, toward an interpretive one. Ethnography in particular has writing as its center (the "graphy" means, after all, writing). This implies more than an incidental method but also implies the partiality of cultural truths. Ethnological fiction "has lost its connotation of falsehood, of something merely opposed to truth. It suggests the partiality of cultural and historical truths, the ways they are systematic and exclusive."[16] True fiction as a method now suggests an analytic understanding rather than solely an empirical one. The point that *Writing Culture* editors were making is that ethnographic writing is a made thing, a fiction in that sense, not in the sense of unable to convey "real" representations.

On the Plaza: A case study

An example of an ethnographic study may be the best way to understand its connection to the concept of a thick description. Setha Low[17] writes such a specific case for Parque Central and Plaza de la Cultura in San Jose, Costa Rica. This book involved work completed intermittently during a period of 20 years. It highlights the variety of methods and the development of an analytic framework. And it is particularly relevant to our interest since it involves architecture and urban design and a linked study of human behavior in these places.

A preliminary personal account includes field notes of conversations and unstructured observation from five separate trips to San Jose from 1985 to 1997. Based on this work, methods including observation, interviews and historical documentation, ethnohistorical archive research, photographic documentation, and developed analysis structure her book. This detailed research leads to an understanding of the sociopolitical and historical context of both plazas including events, changes, and controversies, derived largely from public sources including news accounts and public documents.

This is followed by a general discussion of European plaza design in France and Spain as precedents to Spanish colonialism in Latin America. This is extended by a history of resistance to colonial plazas in Costa Rica by the indigenous Nahua and Maya populations. Under these pressures, the plazas were continuously reconceived, redefined, and reworked. An overview of theories on spatializing culture, including Castells, Foucault, Rabinow, deCerteau, and Lefebvre, provides a framework for understanding the social production of plaza space. A detailed analysis of each plaza begins with a formal description followed by diagramming population counts, movement diagrams, behavioral maps, and time sequences to provide detailed understanding of the use of the plazas.

Plazas are designed and resisted as politically motivated artistic expressions. Public space as a site of protest is uncovered through written evidence in public archives and news reports, including the plaza in Costa Rican literature. Included in the research are five long conversations with people in the plaza, gathering their recollections in unstructured interviews.

The sum of these disparate methods is a thick description of the public space, politics, and democracy in Costa Rica that constitutes an accessible form of local knowledge. Such a wide-ranging description is vital to how ethnography, architecture, and HCI may be able to create a new understanding of architectural settings.

Notes

1 Geertz, Clifford. "Thick description: Toward an interpretive theory of culture." In *The cultural geography reader*, pp. 41–51. Routledge, 2008.
2 Bell, G., and P. Dourish. *Diving a digital future: Mess and mythology*. MIT Press, 2014.
3 Weiser, Mark. "The computer for the 21st century." *Scientific American* 265, no. 3 (1991): 94–105.

4 Winograd, Terry, ed. *Bringing design to software*. ACM, 1996.

5 Dourish, Paul. *The stuff of bits: An essay on the materialities of information*. MIT Press, 2022.

6 Levin, D.Z. and R. Cross. The strength of weak ties you can trust: The mediating role of trust in effective knowledge transfer. *Management Science*, 2004. 50(11): p. 1477–1490.

7 The aware home: A living laboratory for ubiquitous computing research; in Norbert Streitz, Shin'ichi Konomi, and Heinz-Jürgen Burkhardt, eds. *Cooperative buildings: integrating information, organization, and architecture*. Vol. 1370. Springer, 2007.

8 Pedersen, E.R., et al. Tivoli: An electronic whiteboard for informal workgroup meetings. in *Proceedings of the INTERACT'93 and CHI'93 conference on Human factors in computing systems*. 1993. ACM.
Bly, S.A., S.R. Harrison, and S. Irwin, Media spaces: Bringing people together in a video, audio, and computing environment. *Commun. ACM*, 1993. 36: p. 28–46.
Gaver, W.W. The affordances of media spaces for collaboration. in *Proceedings of the 1992 ACM conference on Computer-supported cooperative work*. 1992. ACM.

9 Boellstorff, Tom. *Coming of age in Second Life: An anthropologist explores the virtually human*. Princeton University Press, 2015.

10 Churchill, Elizabeth F., Les Nelson, Laurent Denoue and Andreas Girgensohn. The Plasma Poster Network: Posting Multimedia Content in Public Places. IFIP TC13 International Conference on Human-Computer Interaction (2003).
McDonald, D.W., et al., Proactive displays: Supporting awareness in fluid social environments. *ACM Transactions on Computer-Human Interaction*, 2008. 14(4): 1–31.

11 Geertz, Clifford. *The interpretation of cultures*. Basic books, 1973.

12 Geertz, Clifford. ""From the native's point of view": On the nature of anthropological understanding." *Bulletin of the American Academy of Arts And Sciences*, 1974: 26–45.

13 Dilthey, Wilhelm. *Hermeneutics and the study of history: Selected works, Volume IV*. Edited by R.A. Makkreel and F. Rodi. Princeton University Press, 1996.

14 Spitzer, Leo. "The 'Ode on a Grecian Urn,' or Content vs. Metagrammar." *Comparative Literature* 7, no. 3 (1955): 203–225.

15 Geertz, Clifford. "Blurred genres: The refiguration of social thought." *The American Scholar* (1980): 165–179.

16 Clifford, James, and George E. Marcus, eds. *Writing culture: the poetics and politics of ethnography: a School of American Research advanced seminar*. University of California Press, 1986.

17 Low, Setha M. *On the plaza: The politics of public space and culture*. University of Texas Press, 2000.

5

AFFORDANCE

Ecological and social

J. J. Gibson, in his book *The Ecological Approach to Visual Perception*, presents a clear argument that perception is tightly interconnected with the physical setting within which humans (and all other living things) evolved and exist:

> an affordance is neither an objective property nor a subjective property; or it is both if you like. An affordance cuts across the dichotomy of subjective–objective and helps us to understand its inadequacy. It is equally a fact of the environment and a fact of behavior. It is both physical and psychical, yet neither. An affordance points both ways, to the environment and to the observer.
>
> (p. 121)

We will be examining how this might influence the study of architecture and human–computer interaction (HCI).

There is considerable evidence from neuroscience that people process sensory information along two distinct, parallel pathways in the brain: a "where" pathway, concerned with spatial and functional information about the environment, and a "what" pathway, focusing on object recognition and semantic knowledge.[1] For example, in the case of a person attempting to navigate a spatial environment, the stream of "where" information forms a cognitive map of their surroundings while the "what" pathway collects semantic information in a network structure.

DOI: 10.4324/9781003363392-5

Research in other fields was also interested in the role that space played with perception and memory. For example, the term "cognitive map" was first used by psychologist Edward Tolman in "Cognitive maps in rats and men."[2] He describes a maze previously mastered by rats that is blocked at a critical point and replaced by a series of radially arranged alternatives. The dominant school of strict behaviorism would expect the rats to select random new exits. But in fact the rats greatly prefer the route that demonstrates an understanding of the spatial overview of the maze. Tolman labels this behavior a "cognitive map": "map" indicating the use of a spatial figure and "cognitive" as a usually simplified description that can be held in the brain.

Kevin Lynch's book *Image of the City* develops the idea of a cognitive map from the viewpoint of urban theory.[3] Based on empirical studies of sketch maps by residents of Boston, Jersey City, and Los Angeles, Lynch develops a set of categories, including paths, edges, nodes, districts, and landmarks, that are used in understanding and wayfinding through these urban environments. Lynch's work has been foundational not just within urban studies, but also in a wide variety of fields, as an example of underlying cognitive processes.

Ecological perception

Long before the psychologist J. J. Gibson developed his theory of ecological perception, his first published work dealt with automobile driving with the goal of finding the "field of safe travel."[4] This field is not fixed, but shifts as one moves through space or other cars approach. It is interpreted by the driver who is interested in finding the center of the path of safe travel. This path shifts over time, reacting both physically in the space and through interpretations of possible impediments by the driver. Two options are open to the driver: stopping to avoid a collision or navigating by accelerating, decelerating, or steering toward the path of safe travel (see Figure 5.1). Clearance lines identify a gradient of the future positions of obstacles in the path.

Gibson was already dissatisfied with the dominant gestalt theory of perception, particularly with the insistence that perception was entirely dependent on a process within the mind. He was equally interested in the physical world and the direct perception of it. Following on with this work, Gibson entered the U.S. Army during World War II, where he became the director of a unit for the Army Air Force's Aviation Psychology Program applying the same analysis to the difficult problem of landing aircraft on

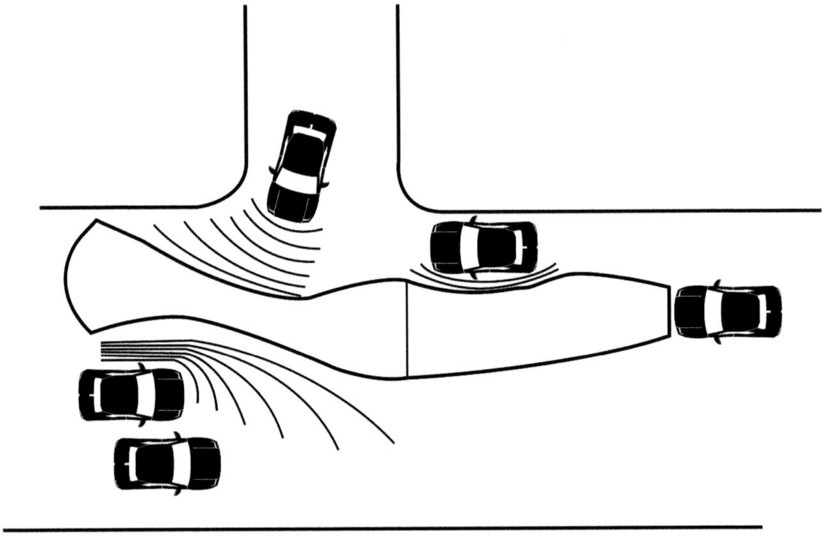

FIGURE 5.1 The field of safe travel and the minimum stopping zone of a driver in traffic.

the rolling deck of an aircraft carrier. His interest was the effect that flight had on visual perception; he influenced both the development of visual aptitude testing used to help with pilot selection and training methods using motion pictures as a tool.

Following the war, Gibson returned to academic research at Cornell and developed an ecological theory of visual perception elaborated through a sequence of three books.

The Perception of the Visual World[5] is an extension of his early work, especially on flight. Unlike earlier gestalt psychologists who focused on perception as an internal mental process, Gibson understands perception as an interaction of the physical world with people's experience of it. He outlines how this perception is direct, rather than based on internal cognitive processes. His emphasis is on what he calls a "ground" theory, a continuous surface or adjacent surfaces upon which visual space is perceived. Motion is central to how an animal perceives the world; as Gibson notes it is motion that differentiates the animal kingdom from the plant kingdom. This leads to his development of optic arrays, based on information sampled from the outside world. He further developed the idea of optical flow, a description of the apparent flow of objects in the visual field relative to the observer.

The Senses Considered as Perceptual Systems[6] studies the organs by which "an organism can take account of its environment and cope with

FIGURE 5.2 Optical flow diagram: The pattern of motion between a person and the objects, surfaces, and edges around them.

objective facts." The auditory, haptic, tasting, smelling, and visual systems are described in evolutionary detail for a number of species, consistent with Gibson's contention that all animals can only be understood simultaneously with their environment. He presents these systems as direct perceptions of the physical world.

The Ecological Approach to Visual Perception,[7] the final book in this sequence, is the most philosophical and complete explanation of his work. All animal species (including humans) have evolved to be adapted to a particular physical setting. Humans evolved as bi-pedal, upright mammals, highly skilled at visual pattern recognition. In contrast, a bird or a mole or a fish is adapted to other niches; the organs of perception have a wide range of abilities.

Gibson insists that the environment and the animal are not separable. He uses the term "ecological niche" to describe the physical attributes where the perceptual apparatus (at first visual for his research) evolved.

He also articulates the importance of motion for animals, either literally moving through space, shifting one's eyes or head, or perceiving it within its view.

He invents the noun "affordance" as a nominalization of the verb "to afford," describing the opportunities for action provided by an object or environment. He understands affordance as an aspect of the physical setting as perceived by a particular animal, not as a cultural construct. Affordances are continuously perceived as meaningful wholes, not as separate elements stitched together, and are perceived more easily than separate qualities. Gibson argued that when we perceive an object we observe the object's affordances and not its particular qualities. He believed that perceiving affordances of an object is easier than perceiving the many different qualities an object may have. Objects may have multiple affordances.

The extensive modifications to the environment that humans have made, such as stairs on steep slopes, are designed to create an affordance for walking where it does not exist.

He lists the aspects of an object's affordance:

- Size: graspable by a human hand, items such as handles or edges.
- Shape: comfortable to a human hand (prehension), smooth to the hand.
- Material: amorphous or transparent objects can resist prehension.
- Texture: spikey or rough texture can resist prehension.
- Distance: object affordance is strongest at easily reachable positions.

Because Gibson was convinced that affordances were immediately perceived in the world, he believed that sound experimentation was possible (or even preferable) in the real world rather than in laboratory conditions.

For environmental psychology, space was fundamentally three dimensional, discoverable through movement. To Gibson, perception is a compilation of the person's environment and how the person interacts with it.

Donald Norman

By far the most widespread impact of Gibson's idea of affordance has been in the work of Donald Norman, notably in the book *The Design of Everyday Things*,[8] which has been cited over 20,000 times. Norman is known as the leading proponent of user centered design, which we discussed in an earlier chapter on HCI (Chapter 3). While the intended audience of the book is the computer science community, the first examples offered in the book are architectural elements: doors and electric switches. Both examples are more directly connected to Gibson's definition of affordance as the intersection of an animal and its environmental niche defined by the physical setting. Norman, however, is intent on extending affordance to include social and cultural aspects of users. So, for example, he is interested in language-based definitions. It is important to be aware of the two definitions of affordance, as each will refer to a different context. But both can be useful tools for design.

Norman's principles that are relevant to architecture include:

- The use of knowledge both in the world and in the head. This involves the designer model, the user model, and the system image as well as simplifying the structure of the task.
- Making things visible to bridge the gap between execution and evaluation.
- Exploit natural mappings, connecting the spatial relationship between the controls and the system.
- Exploit the power of constraints.

Norman's ideas about architecture are most convincing at the scale of elements such as include furniture, plumbing fixtures, cabinets, flooring, and other parts of a building that are intended to be directly in contact with users. It is less convincing at the level of spatial definition, possibly because of his background in computer science focused on devices rather than setting.

Affordance in architectural design

Given its insistence on the importance of linking physical properties in the environment to particular animals for an understanding of perception, affordance has been a tempting idea for designers. J. J. Gibson himself noted as an aside that architecture and design might not have a satisfactory theoretical basis, and then he asks if an ecological approach to the psychology of perception and behavior can provide such a basis.[9] Gibson provided no details, but there have been efforts to develop such a theory of affordance for architectural design. A similar argument has been made by Rietveld[10] based on the abilities of an animal or a human, such as language, that extend the idea of affordance past mere motor-based abilities.

Recent work focused on architectural design[11] distinguishes between building elements and spaces as possible sites for the use of affordance theory during the design process. Building elements are at a scale that is usually directly touched (or grasped to use Gibson's term) by users. Spaces are less susceptible to Norman's analysis, although they are primary examples of Gibson's interest in level surfaces that afford walking for humans. There is some overlap with professional handbooks such as (*Time-Saver Standards for Building Types*) that provide details of spatial arrangements at several scales ranging from the site to furniture layout for standard building types.[12] Some work has been attempted to use opening between spaces and diagramming of functions with spaces. Affordance can integrate this information over the entire life cycle of a building. A main advantage of this method is during the design process as a way of extending the architect's perception.

Previous work on pattern language by Chis Alexander[13] specifically aimed to integrate all relevant information (spatial, acoustic, constructional, social, etc.) within a specific physical location in a building. These patterns can then be used as a web of relationships for design. An example of a pattern (staircase as a stage 133) includes reference to the human use of the stair as a place to site, its position within the larger room, the stairs'relationship to the front door, as well as the ergonomic and constructional implications of tread, riser, and handrail design. This description is the grammar of the pattern. Each pattern is related to some of the other 253 patterns which vary widely in scale and focus. This pattern is related to stair seats (125), Zen view (134), tapestry of light and dark (135), staircase volume (195), and the shape of indoor space (194); the set of relationships create a syntax of patterns. Due to various factors, Alexander's approach has seen diminishing influence in architecture. However, his work is widely used in computer science, having been applied to software design patterns and interaction design patterns. Wiki, the online encyclopedia, was explicitly patterned on pattern language.[14]

Another approach to the structure of architectural space is Bill Hillier's work on space syntax.[15] A convex map of a building can be created where rooms and doorways are treated as separate spaces and adjacent accesses as links. This is much less useful than his urban analysis that deals directly with views in the open space of the exterior space of a city that has been used to define measures (integration, betweenness, and scale) of particular street segments. Benedikt's work on isovists[16] explicitly relies on Gibson's description of the visual field defined by the location of an observer and the ability to see across a flat field. Isovists can be used as an algorithm that can compute a value for any particular location; when used as a grid of viewpoints of variable density within a building it creates a measure and graphic representation of visibility for the interior space. By implementing isovists across many points within a building it can help to capture the impact of movement through the building.

Some work has also been done on a simulation program for motion through architectural space that explicitly addresses Gibson's concept of ecological perception based on optic arrays. Using interactive and agent-based methods, affordance-based control of perceptually guided action is linked to enable a simulation for movement.[17]

Withagen and Caljouw[18] analyzed Aldo van Eyck's urban playground in Amsterdam in light of affordance. These playgrounds built on small sites within the city are not fenced and separated from adjoining spaces.

FIGURE 5.3 Three playgrounds designed by Aldo van Eyck at different locations in Amsterdam. Images courtesy of Amsterdam City Archive; reprinted with permission.

The placement of simple geometric elements (rather than predetermined equipment) within the space is meant to encourage multiple engagements; the same object can be used to sit on, to walk on, or to jump from one to another. In Gibson's terms they afford multiple engagements, for van Eyck they were tools for imagination. A further analysis of the placement of simple elements (stepping stones) revealed more engagement when a variety of spacing was present.[19]

Salingaros[20] suggests a connection between Gibson's concept of affordance and Alexander and Pallasmaa.[21] He suggests the need for graspable "handles" to be physically present, or at least suggested in our immediate environment. He further claims that modernist architecture, using plate-glass curtain walls and minimalist surfaces, fails to provide such handles. Physical built elements and designs suggestive of grasping (e.g. moldings, ornament, and trim) are common in traditional and vernacular methods of construction and provide such "handles" that connect a direct understanding of affordances.

Meanwhile, a few other researchers have begun to apply the concept of affordance to architectural design explicitly. Tweed (2001)[22] reports progress on identifying and highlighting affordances within computer-aided architectural design (CAAD) software. Koutamanis (2006)[23] follows Norman's application of the concept of affordance to individual building elements such as door handles, and proceeds to apply affordances to architectural spaces in which he introduces the technique of "affordance mapping" to help architects think about the affordances of their architectural designs. In a similar vein, Kim et al. (2008)[24] study the actual affordances of a building lobby and how they vary between different users. Whereas the above authors tend to focus on techniques for using the concept of affordance in architecture, our focus in this chapter is a thorough application of affordances on a theoretical level which should underlie subsequent practical applications.

Maier has proposed[25] that affordance can serve as a basis and framework for architectural theory, design, and practice. Affordance ties together human occupants and the built environment and explains behavior. Maier develops two distinct types of affordances for buildings. First are artifact–user affordances which express a complementary relationship between two separate systems combining the built environment (artifact) and the human occupants (users). These always are expressed as a complementary pair. Artifact–artifact affordances express a relationship between two (or more) subsystems in which a behavior can manifest between the two subsystems that either one cannot manifest in isolation. For example multiple artifacts (e.g. walls affording support to roofs, sprinklers affording suppression of fires) create additional affordance by their combination. This scheme can

FIGURE 5.4 "The End of Sitting." Amsterdam 2014. An installation by RAAAF using affordance theory to solicit visitors to explore different standing positions in an experimental work landscape.

create a broad framework uniting the work and understanding of architects, engineers, future occupants, and other stakeholders. Such a framework will also facilitate knowledge capture and re-use.

Rietveld[26] has directly connected research on affordance with a built proposal titled "The End of Sitting," an installation at the crossroads of visual art, architecture, philosophy, and empirical science. The environment has been designed for sitting, but medical research suggests that too much sitting has adverse health effects. Rietveld Architecture–Art Affordances (RAAAF) have explored a concept eliminating the chair and desk as the inevitable starting points. Instead, the installation's various affordances solicit visitors to explore different standing positions in an experimental work landscape. "The End of Sitting" proposes a radical change in the working environment. Experimentation determined optimal angles for support of the upper body while standing, leaning, and reclining. This carved landscape integrates many affordances for standing and allows people to work while being supported by the material structure of the environment. It is one of the few examples of specific designs that attempts to put affordance theory into architectural practice.

Notes

1 Aguirre, G.K. and D'Esposito, M. "Environmental knowledge is subserved by separable dorsal/ventral neural areas." *Journal of Neuroscience*, 17(7) (1997): 2512–2518. Goodale, M.A. and Milner, A.D. "Separate visual pathways for perception and action." *Trends in Neuroscience*, 15(1) (1992): 20–25. Kaas, J.H. and Hackett, T.A. 2000. "What" and "where" processing in auditory cortex. *Nature Neuroscience*, 2(12), 1045–1047.

2 Tolman, E.C., 1948. Cognitive maps in rats and men. *Psychological Review, 55*(4), p. 189.

3 Lynch, K. *The image of the city*. MIT Press, 1964.

4 Gibson, J.J. and Crooks, L.E., 1938. A theoretical field-analysis of automobile-driving. *The American Journal of Psychology, 51*(3), pp. 453–471.

5 Gibson, J.J., 1950. The perception of the visual world. Houghton Mifflin Company.

6 Gibson, J.J., 1966. The senses considered as perceptual systems. Houghton Mifflin Company.

7 Gibson, J.J., 1979. The ecological approach to visual perception. Psychology Press.

8 Norman, Don. *The design of everyday things: Revised and expanded edition*. Basic books, 2013.

9 Maier, Jonathan R.A., Georges M. Fadel, and Dina G. Battisto. "An affordance-based approach to architectural theory, design, and practice." *Design Studies* 30, no. 4 (2009): 393-414.

10 Rietveld, Erik, and Julian Kiverstein. "A rich landscape of affordances." *Ecological psychology* 26, no. 4 (2014): 325–352.

11 Koutamanis, Alexander. "Buildings and affordances." In Design computing and cognition'06 Ed. JS Gero, pp. 345-364. Dordrecht: Springer Netherlands, 2006.

12 Joseph De Chiara, and Michael J. Crosbie. Time-Saver Standards for Building Types. McGraw-Hill, 2001. These are now largely superseded by online resources such as the *Whole Building Design Guide* https://Www.Wbdg.Org/. Accessed July 26, 2023.
13 Alexander, Christopher. *A pattern language: Towns, buildings, construction*. Oxford University Press, 1977.
14 Cunningham, Ward, and Michael W. Mehaffy. "Wiki as pattern language." In Proceedings of the 20th Conference on Pattern Languages of Programs (PLoP'13), Monticello, IL, USA, pp. 23-26. 2013.
15 Hillier, Bill. *Space is the machine: a configurational theory of architecture*. Space Syntax, 2007.
16 Benedikt, Michael L. "To take hold of space: isovists and isovist fields." Environment and Planning B: Planning and design 6, no. 1 (1979): 47–65.
17 Braund, Michael and Daniel Hambleton. "Dragonfly: An Ecological Approach to Digital Architectural Design." ACADIA proceedings. 2011.
18 Withagen, Rob, and Simone R. Caljouw. "Aldo van Eyck's playgrounds: Aesthetics, affordances, and creativity." *Frontiers in Psychology* 8 (2017): 1130.
19 Sporrel, Karlijn, Simone R. Caljouw, and Rob Withagen. "Gap-crossing behavior in a standardized and a non standardized jumping stone configuration." PLoS One 12, no. 5 (2017): e0176165.
20 Salingaros, Nikos. "Why we need to "grasp" our surroundings: Object affordance and prehension in architecture." Journal of Architecture and Urbanism 41, no. 3 (2017): 163–169.
21 Pallasmaa, Juhani. The eyes of the skin: Architecture and the senses. John Wiley & Sons, 2012.
22 Tweed, Christopher. "The social context of CAAD in practice." *Automation in Construction* 10, no. 5 (2001): 617-629.
23 Koutamanis, Alexander. "Buildings and affordances." In *Design computing and cognition'06*, pp. 345-364. Dordrecht: Springer Netherlands, 2006.
24 Kim, Yong Se, Min Kyoung Kim, Ji Yun Jeong, and Jae Ho Moon. "Study on personal characteristics and emotional affordances through user activity analysis." In *Proc. Design and Emotion Conf., Hong Kong, October*, pp. 6-9. 2008.
25 Maier, Jonathan RA, Georges M. Fadel, and Dina G. Battisto. "An affordance-based approach to architectural theory, design, and practice." Design Studies 30, no. 4 (2009): 393–414.
26 Rietveld, Erik. "Situating the embodied mind in a landscape of standing affordances for living without chairs: materializing a philosophical worldview." Sports Medicine 46, no. 7 (2016): 927–932.

6

MOVEMENT AND POSITION

In her book *Le Corbusier and the Architectural Promenade,* Flora Samuel cites Le Corbusier's comment about the centrality of movement for the experience of architecture:

> Architecture is experienced as one roams about in it and walks through it ... So true is this that architectural works can be divided into dead and living ones depending on whether the law of "roaming through" has not been observed or whether on the contrary it has been brilliantly obeyed.[1]

And as Walter Benjamin noted, "architecture has always represented the prototype of a work of art the reception of which is consummated by a collectivity in a state of distraction" (p. 13).[2] J. J. Gibson has remarked on the way in which movement and its correlate, position, are intuitively connected to the perception of space. And we will see in this chapter how sensing motion in buildings can be accomplished anonymously, democratically, and efficiently.

Within architecture, circulation has always been a central organizing principle for design and occupation; the pivotal role of floor plans in architectural representation focuses on exactly this issue.

This is particularly evident when an architect focuses attention on unique aspects of circulation. For example, the Vestibule of the Laurentian Library by Michelangelo is a mannerist composition of a wide, flowing, tripartite staircase and a palace facade stuffed into a cramped space. The Apollolaan School in Amsterdam by Hertzberger is an elementary school overflowing

DOI: 10.4324/9781003363392-6

into and occupying a stair that also serves as a series of niches for students, elaborate thresholds to classrooms, and serves as an assembly space for the entire school. The combination of a stair and ramp in the Illinois Institute of Technology (IIT) Student Union by Rem Koolhaas creates a unique interior landscape navigation between the new building and the original Mies dining pavilion. The Villa Savoye threads open stairs and ramps through the villa to see to and from (see Figure 6.1).

Burning Man/Black Rock City

Some spatial settings address movement more systematically. The Burning Man festival at Black Rock City in the remote desert of northwest Nevada[3] is a carefully planned temporary city approximately 1.5 miles in diameter organized in a concentric grid occupying 240 degrees of an arc focused on a common area named Center Camp. Burning Man has been described as a "techno hippie carnival … which later turned into something of a sprawling frat party for the technogentsia."[4] The festival features large scale interactive installation art (including "mutant vehicles") often with kinetic, electronic, and fire elements. This ephemeral city has always served as a way to spatially frame the activities of Burning Man. And Burning Man is also framed in time; it has a clearly defined beginning and end. Black Rock City is also unique for its extreme remoteness from other human settlements that requires an eight-hour pilgrimage from San Francisco. Black Rock City also demands a particular kind of attention, providing a particular setting in which the art lives, is enacted, and is part of the follower's experience.

Black Rock City provides not only isolation and focusing, but is also a complex and extensive urban network. The experience of a city as large and heterogeneous as Black Rock City is inevitably episodic, recalling Guy Debord's goal for psychogeography as a means of renewing our ability to experience the city directly and without preconception.[5] The layout of Black Rock City began with a reference to gathering around the campfire,[6] with the burning man sculpture (set on fire at the conclusion of each festival) at the center of a circular street grid intersected by radial streets. The rigid geometry, reminiscent of Brazilia or a Roman military encampment, was largely dictated by access requirements from the Bureau of Land Management for issuance of a permit.

The experience of Burning Man belies what could be an oppressive regularity of the grid. The distinction between the rational organization of the streets is in high contrast to the rich variety of installations, sculpture, and art projects placed in the city: an unending *passegiatta*. These installations

FIGURE 6.1 Top: Villa Savoye, Le Corbusier, stair and ramp at center of villa (image courtesy of scarletgreen). Bottom: Interior of the Amsterdamse Montessori School. Apolloscholen, Amsterdam, the Netherlands (1980–1983). Architect: Herman Hertzberger (© Herman Hertzberger).

FIGURE 6.2 An aerial view of Black Rock City. Image: Courtesy of Jay Allen (https://www.flickr.com/photos/jayallen/240600283).

display little of the regularity evident on most urban streets, often dictated by legal or quasi-legal restrictions on building placement. Most of the camps and installations in Black Rock City are free standing objects that do little to define the edges of the streets. The emphasis on radical self-expression guarantees a wide variety of sizes, locations, materials, styles, forms, and activities. Moving along the 13 curvilinear streets is experienced as an unfolding panorama of energetic or even riotous heterogeneity. The only clear visual organization that is apparent at ground level are the radial streets focused on the Burning Man statue at the center.

Dancing about architecture[7]

A joint project between Eric Sauda and dance professor Dr. Kaustavi Sarkar explored the intersection of architectural design, dance choreography, and technological mediation. Collaborative groups of advanced dance and architecture students created interactive settings and choreographed performances via the mediation of software and hardware including modul8, Kinect motion capture, and video projection. This work was presented to an audience from both departments, including expert outside reviewers in both disciplines. The settings for this work were intentionally challenging to performance norms and ranged from lobby spaces to a gallery to classrooms. Calling on the dancers' proprioceptive awareness, choreographic techniques included distortions of static spatial planes created by ethereal biomorphic membranes, the use of Kinect motion capture and choreography

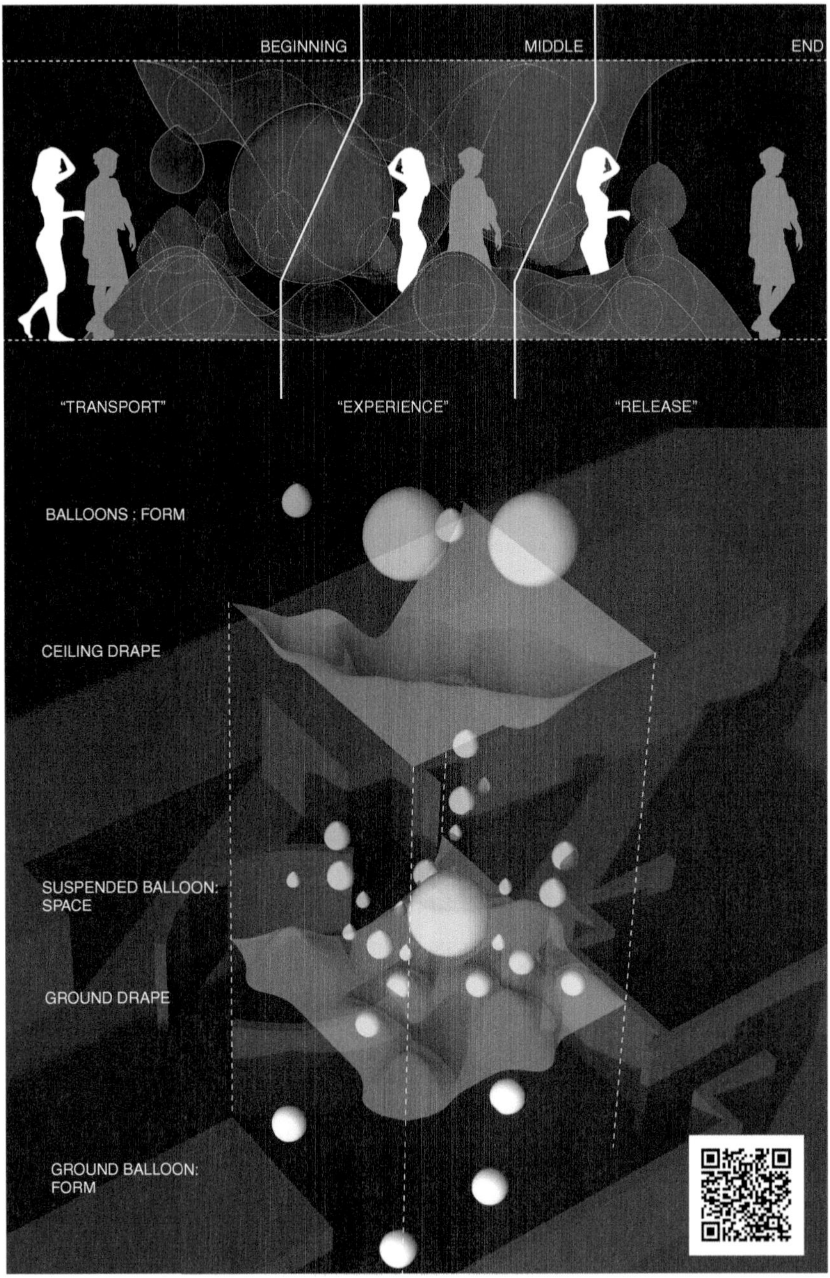

FIGURE 6.3 Dancing about architecture: An interactive movement based performance by Eric Sauda et al.

based on call and response between reality and the digital self, the forced participation of the audience members in the dance, and the creation of spatial separation between dancers and audience. The viewing/participating audience members in these durational, interactive, and concert-style presentations become a part of the choreography while figuring out their relationships with the multiple components of the dance, the technology, and the interactive components. These techniques enable a negotiation between disciplines where dance needs to make space for architecture and architecture needs to move itself to fit into dancing shoes.

The Space Between is one example of this work. The mixed media installation in the public lobby of an academic building included two layers of plastic sheets warped around large scale balloons at three levels. The ceiling balloons are attached to the ceiling and covered with the first sheet of plastic. The middle layer of balloons will enable the projection and digital interactivity, responding to the sound of popping balloons and vibrating their images in and out of focus. Balloons were also attached to the floor, covered by the second layer of plastic as well as fans and a fog machine. The dancers guide the audience individually in silence through the biomorphic membranes immersed by the sounds, visuals, and interactivity of the set, and then release them back to the static space outside the set. The movement through the lobby, typically experienced in a state of distraction, is in this case through the agency of the specific skills of the dancers, raised to the level of consciousness for each member of the audience.

Digital movement data systems: Foundations

Given the rapidly expanding ability to automate the collection of data about human occupation in architectural settings, there has been growing interest in techniques available that may help in analysis and decision making. Architects have long relied solely on precedent and assumptions to define how their designs impact human occupation and use. Before examining contemporary examples of approaches to this problem, we need to establish some foundational issues within the field, which we will call intelligent architectural settings. The goal of intelligent architectural settings is to employ sensing technologies of all types to collect large archives of data about human occupation and to employ data science analytic techniques to better understand and transform those settings.

Automated sensing can detect movement using a range of technologies. The precision, complexity, and security of these technologies vary greatly, but they can all be referenced to a common spatial representation. Sensing devices have become relatively miniaturized, inexpensive, and common throughout architectural settings. These devices range from motion sensors to simple Radio Frequency Identification (RFID) tags to Bluetooth beacons to camera arrays. Specially designed devices such as identity badges offer individual user data, but are often difficult for settings without homogeneous user groups. Passive sensing such as motion detectors and cameras can gather information about a much wider group without the need to recruit participants. An overlapping choice is between specific devices engineered for a study versus connection to an existing device such as a smartphone. While smartphones are tempting as sensing devices, there are significant problems with differing platforms and low levels of participation. Less intrusive devices such as Bluetooth beacons do not provide a consistent signal and have difficulty registering relative locations through walls as they rely on triangulation to locate an individual's device in a space.

Privacy has become a major concern for all systems that gather information about human occupants. In many settings, users may have significant objections to the retention of data. In health care facilities, there are legal requirements that constrain the use of patient data, but such guarantees are scarce for employees, and can be a source of considerable concern and resistance. A strategy for protecting and engaging the users of the system and assuring them of the limits of the use of the collected data will be important to the success of any intelligent architectural setting. Such safeguards are particularly important for sensing such as ID tags that are inherently connected to an individual. One important method to maintain privacy is through strategies to anonymize information. For sensors that are intrinsically identified with a user (such as employee ID tags), this can require an affirmative decision to discard certain portions of the data to gain the confidence of the users. Interestingly, for computer vision systems, extraction of vector information from video footage is the only practical way to compress the enormous size of video files, though individual user identification is not intrinsic to the current systems. This provides some temporary privacy now, but as technology advances this is likely to become a recurrent issue.

There is considerable variation in the expectation of privacy in different settings. Within a home, the expectation of privacy is very high, and most employees have come to understand that they have limited privacy at work. Public spaces are a more nuanced setting, where expectations of privacy depend on the activities performed there and the timing of events. Finally, there are settings, such as memory care units and autism classrooms, where observation is an expectation and desire of the client and privacy is a minor concern.

Inclusiveness is the flip side of concerns about privacy. Systems that are aimed only at specific, well-defined groups such as employees of a single company or students in defined classroom settings have a very different set of issues from those aimed at more heterogeneous groups such as people in public lobbies or using a transit system. Particularly with the distinction between wearable sensors and passive sensing, many sensors can be difficult to implement broadly across large groups of disparate users of a particular space. It is generally a goal to include as many users as possible in studies, but this constitutes particular challenges to approaches that emphasize custom sensors.

Analytic techniques are equally as important as sensing. While the results of studying architectural settings have progressed from simple counting and qualitative assessments of limited applicability, the flood of new data that will come from new sensing technology will require a more sophisticated understanding of the analysis of large-scale data. Data returned from sensors can be analyzed for frequency and type using tabulations and comparison. There are many existing programs for comparing this data, which are typically built into the control software for the device. In architectural settings, location is an obvious interest, and the use of graphics to identify spatial location is a particularly powerful tool. Work by researchers including Edward Tufte demonstrates how to use graphics as a powerful tool of understanding.[8] In the field of visualization, the development of graphic tools capable of linking data between multiple windows showing different representations of the same data facilitated a deeper exploration of complex datasets. Such visualizations enable one to see patterns in data differently, and to engage "visual thinking." The ability to interact with data visualization is a particularly powerful way to allow users at all levels of expertise to explore and question the meaning of the data. The field of visual analytics has made rapid advances that are particularly suited to the analysis of architectural settings. A technique used in computer science research allows supervised learning by machines that search for recurrent patterns across large time frames or large collections of data. No examples currently exist for architecture, but this method is clearly suitable for spatial analysis.

Research goals for architecture settings can vary in significant ways and are likely to continue to evolve as new opportunities arise. The most straightforward application of data from architectural settings is the evaluation and improvement of building design. This will require the analysis of multiple settings or a single setting over an extended period of time, both of which are or may become feasible using sensing technology and advanced analytic methods. It will also require the construction of data archives that hold the promise of reasonably anticipating human behavior in a variety of settings. As these archives expand, they hold the promise of improving performance in measurable ways. This could be particularly important in areas such as hospital and office design that have defined functions and measurable outcomes.

Intelligent architecture settings may evolve that connect an understanding of human behavior with a knowledge of time and location. It may be possible to develop a thick description: as Clifford Geertz describes it, the difference between "a wink and a blink." Such a paradigm proposes the creation of "intelligent" architectural settings that capture such meaningful behavior in real time and generate knowledge that is useful both in the real world and as an interface with the users.

Emerging models

The collection of data about human occupation has been explored in a variety of venues and contexts as technology has become more integrated. The so-called Internet of Things has created a groundswell of cheaper and more reliable methods for interacting with our environment through wireless sensors. These sensors have often been adapted to monitor the comfort, use, and occupation of space. The following are a subset of some of the explorations undertaken by designers and researchers to better understand the occupation of our environment.

Smart thermostats and smart homes

Smart thermostats are Wi-Fi-connected devices that can be used with home automation and are responsible for controlling a home's heating, ventilation, and air conditioning. They perform similar functions as a programmable thermostat as they allow the user to control the temperature of their home throughout the day using a schedule, but also contain additional features, such as sensors and Wi-Fi connectivity,[9] that are improvements.

In an attempt to mitigate the issues with human error involved with programmable thermostats, the smart thermostat utilizes a sensor that can determine occupancy patterns to automatically change the temperature based on occupant patterns and behaviors. The nest learning thermostat in particular uses passive infrared (PIR) motion sensors inside the unit to sense occupancy in the vicinity. In the case where the home is not occupied, the thermostat can suspend heating/cooling until the sensor is reactivated by an occupant. This sensor is also used to determine the occupancy patterns to create the auto schedule. A grille is placed in front of the sensor to visually conceal and protect the PIR motion sensor inside the thermostat. The grille also helps to make the thermostat visually pleasing.[10] While this sensor technology is important for conserving energy, it is not without flaws. One of the major issues is that the sensor must be activated by someone walking in front of or near the thermostat. It is possible that an occupant could be at home and not pass in front of the sensor. In this case, the thermostat would shut off the heating/cooling and decrease human comfort.

This discussion of smart thermostats is indicative of the larger field of smart homes, which are understood in HCI as an extension of ubiquitous computing extending "smartness" into dwellings for comfort, healthcare, safety, security, and energy conservation. Telecommunication and web connected technologies are central to this effort. Research on smart homes has focused on comfort, healthcare, and security.[11] Technology focused publications greatly outnumber all others. The preponderance of technological research is also due to the straightforward objective evaluation of factors such as temperature, energy consumption, and lighting levels.[12]

Human dynamics laboratory

Alex Pentland leads the Human Dynamics Laboratory at MIT whose mission is to use data to better understand human society.[13] Ben Waber's work at Sociometrics Solutions grew out of this work and has been used by a number of large corporations to better understand and improve the performance of their employees. Waber coined the term "people analytics" to describe the use of individual sensing devices and the resulting data analysis in business organizations.[14]

The current sensing technology used for this approach is the sociometer badge, which is about the size of a deck of cards and has an IR transmitter, a Bluetooth radio, an accelerometer, and a microphone.[15] The sociometric badge also has on board data processing, which allows it to keep features of conversations (volume, duration, location, etc.) rather than complete audio files. They are capable of recording 40 hours of activity between recharging. The data from the sensors are identified with individual users, and data from multiple individuals can be aggregated. Sociometric badges and their predecessors have been in use since 2000.

Privacy is a particularly important issue within corporate workplace settings. Workers have rightly become anxious about their lack of privacy, and the adoption of sociometric data will rely on strategies that address this issue. Sandy Pentland proposes three concepts important to privacy:[16] opt-in (no data collection without consent), individual control (no use of data for control of users), and data for others only in aggregated form (allows management decisions only to improve working methods).

The studies conducted by Waber are at a larger scale than other research in this field, and his approach demonstrates the implementation of privacy standards without compromising the usefulness of the aggregated data. Indeed, the privacy standards help with the widespread adoption of the sociometric badges, enabling the data to provide a more holistic understanding of occupation and use than individual sensors can. The corporate settings studied by Waber[17] are all subject to considerable control by a central authority. The work settings open the possibility of uniform behavior and technologies across the entire population. It is not clear how they might translate to more heterogeneous, public settings or settings with less control.

Pentland has demonstrated in a research setting how the use of sociometric badges would be useful in analyzing behavior. Waber's work in corporate settings is much more explicit about the ways tracking behavior can lead to better business outcomes. A good example is his work with a Bank of America call center, uncovering the ways in which changes to existing schedules of how employees take breaks from work led to increased retention and performance.

The goal of this research at the human dynamics lab is broadly focused on the understanding of data and human behavior. As it has been developed by Waber, it has focused on improving performance in complex settings through the analysis of behavior. The process emphasizes the collection of data followed by an analysis of meaning, leading to proposed improvements. Waber presents profitability as the primary driver for improving employee comfort and happiness and therefore efficiency.

Space Utilization Study/AECOM

AECOM is a multinational engineering and architecture firm with offices worldwide and approximately 95,000 employees. The firm has a history of time utilization studies dating back to the 1990s that has resulted in a database of over 10 million observations.[18] The data for this is a time log of the use of identified spaces in a variety of building types. Using this data with their clients has enabled them to compare sectors by country, work cultures, and use sectors.

Space Utilization Study (SUS) is a proprietary tool to help clients understand how space is being used and to identify types of activities. There is no automated sensing associated with this approach. The methodology is an adaptation of post-occupancy evaluation techniques. A temporary worker is provided with a tablet and given a fixed route through a facility, with route stops identified for detailed recording. Typically, the observer walks these routes eight times a day over two weeks. At each route stop, a record is entered from a preset list into the tablet of the activity (empty, temporarily unoccupied, collaboration, individual work, pausing), equipment (desktop, laptop, telephone, paper teleconference, tablet, projector), and number of people (1–10). The data collected with SUS is inherently anonymous, so privacy concerns are not a major issue. There is a tradeoff between the time required for data collection and inclusiveness with this approach. It requires no special technology by the user populations, but the manual nature of the data collection limits the number of spaces and the length of time that can be observed. Based on this data, it is possible to examine the change in utilization over time and between spaces. Data can be aggregated for multiple spaces.

The major research goal is the development of a large database that can be searched for similarities and differences. The strength of this approach is the ability to make post-occupancy evaluations routine so that it is possible to conduct them on a more regular basis and incorporate them into changes in the spatial arrangement and scheduling of spaces. This approach also allows customization of the study to include space, activities, or equipment that is of particular interest. One shortcoming is the limit to the number of surveys that can be conducted; it is hard to imagine using this technique for more than an occasional survey. Another shortcoming is the prescriptive nature of the investigations: the survey must be designed to find a precise form of behavior, with little opportunity to observe behavior and new metrics, nor can it provide interpretative data about the user's attitude towards the space or other users in the space.

Case/WeWork

The firm Case was launched in May 2008 with a plan to bring better technology and information flow to the process of designing and constructing a building. Founders and architects Federico Negro, David Fano, and Steve Sanderson saw an opportunity to consult through the entire process (with the help of technology) to streamline efficiency and save money.

Case has recently studied the use of Bluetooth beacons as a method of providing positioning information inside the work space to create a better understanding of the ways in which people use space. Bluetooth beacons connected to a user's cellphone allow for the identification of position information, recorded at regular intervals, which can be varied by the system's operator or the user. The beacons are placed on walls throughout a work environment, typically at least three per room, to afford triangulation of a user's device while they are in a particular room. Beacons can calculate approximate distances and direction from the device and use those measurements from multiple beacons to triangulate a user's location. The signal strength can be distorted by walls, depending upon the density of their makeup and this can often result in anomalies in the data. Placing more beacons throughout the space can allow for fewer anomalies and minimize their impact on the data collected. Case has conducted experiments in their own offices with willing participants (which, given the emphasis of the firm, includes all employees). For a single employee on one day, they collected 3,849 data points (which include spatial information), 589 feet of travel, and 7 hours and 55 minutes in the office. The resulting data can be aggregated and used to create graphic representations of an individual employee's day. Because of the small scale of this approach, issues of privacy have not yet been addressed. It will probably be most effective in small to medium enterprises that have a common mission. The data gathered can be used to create timeline studies of individual users and aggregations of multiple users incorporating time and spatial location. Working with Mani Williams, a PhD student from Rensselaer Polytechnic Institute (RPI) who held a research residency in the firm, they have developed a way to aggregate multiple users movement and position, and develop interactive visualizations using linked windows representing views of the data in spatial temporal and categorical views.[19]

The goal of the research is to create a corpus of data about the movement of users within a space. This data can be used either to improve the efficient use of the space or at a large scale to compare space for their pattern of use. The work at WeWork is currently experimental. The strength of this approach is the automatic way in which it collects information. The data are currently limited to user identification and a spatial location. The firm has not yet faced issues of privacy and widespread adoption within large, potentially heterogeneous settings.

Visual Analytics for Large Scale Ethnography (VALSE)

VALSE is a prototype for a computer-vision-based analytic system developed by a collaborative research group that includes Dr. Scott Spurlock, Dr. Richard Souvenir from computer science, Eric Sauda and Chris Beorkrem from architecture, and the anthropologist Donna Lanclos at UNC Charlotte.[20]

VALSE is intended to serve as a next-level tool capable of providing not only location information for a user, but also to map the behavior of users in a space over very long periods of time. This is an interactive visual analytic system that allows a researcher to identify a behavior that is important to the performance or use of a space and then search a database of the past movement to identify other iterations of this behavior. The tool can then report back frequency, duration, and location of those behaviors since the system was installed. Additionally, the system through machine learning could begin to identify other behaviors that researchers may not

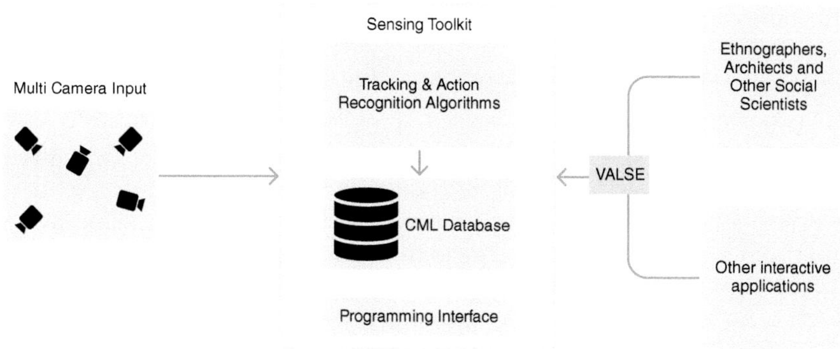

FIGURE 6.4 Diagram of the system architecture for the Sensing Toolkit.

Notes: This will provide an Application Programming Interface (API) for applications to analyze and respond to activity in large spaces. VALSE is built upon the Toolkit which provides tools for visualizing and annotating motions.

have noticed occurring in the space, because of a lack of frequency or because of the subtleness of movement.

Recent advances in computer vision have brought automated analysis of human motion within reach. The Sensing Toolkit is a framework for collecting and storing long-term, large-scale, human motion designed to use a computer vision system, including a network of cameras installed in large indoor spaces, such as building lobbies.[21] The system uses ray-tracing logic to triangulate locations, track movement, and collect metrically accurate locations of where people have been over time, as well as identifying activities that were undertaken while they occupied a location. All of these data are collected while protecting the anonymity of the user by never recording their actual image. Instead the data are saved as a skeletal model consisting of a simplified stick figure representing the human skeleton (a graph of joints connected by bones) which uses a tiny fraction of the space storage required by video.

To facilitate analysis over very long time frames, an interactive, visual analysis interface called VALSE allows domain experts to query and understand the data. VALSE follows a many-coordinated-views paradigm to present a user with motion summaries such as heat maps, scatter plots, and motion trails, as well as avatar-based, animated reconstructions of activity. These visualizations can be dynamically customized with user-defined time intervals for targeted analysis, and replayed using a familiar Digital Video Recorder (DVR) style interface. This type of tool can expand the reach of traditional social science analysis. VALSE leverages the ability of human ethnographers to recognize meaningful patterns of behavior with the computational ability to apply these insights over very extended periods of time.

Large-scale analysis of human behavior in architectural settings requires an understanding of more complex activities than simple gestures. For example, the sequence of a person waving, then walking towards another person, then stopping may correspond to the behavior "meeting a familiar person." Methods for detecting atomic human actions (e.g. walking, waving) from video have become increasingly accurate; however, there has been less success at recognizing activities (e.g. meeting, dancing, studying).

Chapter 4 provided a general introduction to applied ethnography as a research method for architectural settings. Ethnography provides an analytical method of seeing culturally and socially situated practices.[22] Architectural settings become places by virtue of the interactions that take place in them, and the meanings inscribed upon those spaces in the course of those interactions. A critical step in for VALSE is to get at the meaning of those places and interactions.

As a background to developing the VALSE tool, regular observations within a university library served as a model,[23] providing qualitative descriptive data of the contexts and content of the interactions. Structured interview questions arising from the observation data created a cycle of interviews and observations. The interview texts as well as the observation notes were analyzed and coded, informing the design of the VALSE toolkit and its adaptations, serving as ground truth to test the toolkit and measure the impact of the technology in the spaces. In turn, the deployment of the toolkit enables researchers to examine meaningful behavior at a scale not possible without automated tools.

VALSE uses a data-driven approach for learning behaviors from gestures. Domain-specific data (e.g. people moving through a lobby) contain common, repeated, and related motion patterns. Base gestures enable learning higher-level behaviors using data stream mining methods. The Episode Discovery algorithm[24] is used to find overrepresented gesture sequences in large data collections and discover clusters of interactions that are closely related in time and apply significance testing on discovered clusters to generate sets of significant *episodes* based on the frequency of occurrence, length, and regularity. This data-driven approach is used to learn new behaviors that will likely correspond to a single semantic concept. Higher-order models are created by encoding the discovered sequences of gestures and continuing to build a hierarchy of behavior patterns. In addition to validation of automatically discovered behaviors, investigators can use the visual analytics tools to identify motion behaviors of interest. By selecting an example of a motion or activity pattern from video, its constituent gestures can be used as the definition of a new motion motif. Collectively,

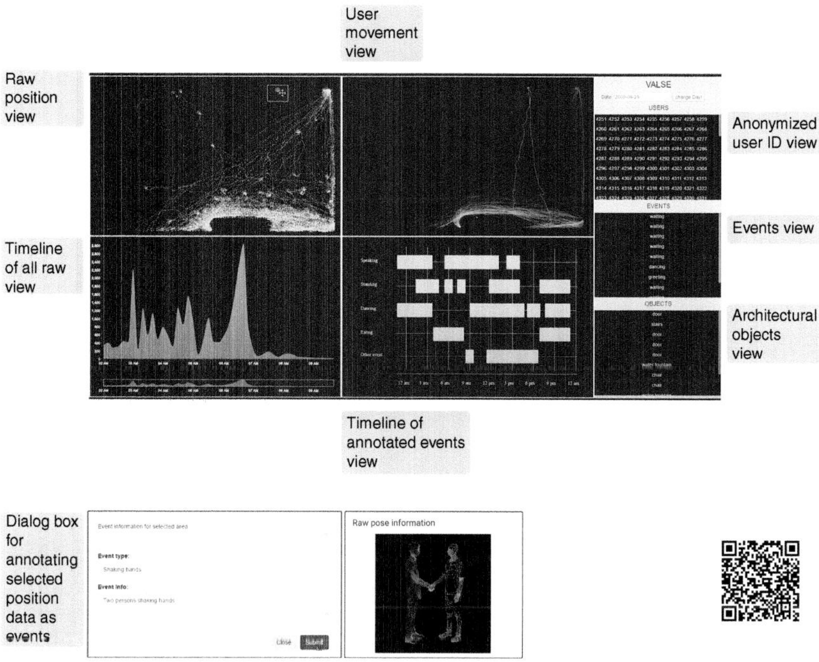

FIGURE 6.5 Prototype of VALSE interface combining timeline visualization with spatial visualizations overlaid with the motion of occupants.

these tools support the aim of having a user, untrained in computer vision, define and query for problem-specific motifs of complex behavior.

Combining computer vision and ethnography into the VALSE system offers the opportunity to understand behavior in architectural settings in a meaningful way over long time frames, including the possibility of real-time understanding and response. The combination of human insight from ethnographers and the computational extension from computer vision is a powerful example of a human–computer analytic system.

VALSE offers the ability to gather detailed data on how human behavior is affected by the design strategy employed in a particular space. Designers have often used spatial and programmatic organizational strategies to justify experimentations in architectural form. For the first time it could monitor the results of these experiments and evaluate their results. This offers the possibility to create a broad analysis of design intentions. Imagine a high school design that can actually be analyzed for its ability to encourage positive and engaging behavior from its students and teachers, and that can be generalized over hundreds of design examples. Particularly those architectural sub-fields that build multiple instances of a common design would be able to learn from each new design and improve subsequent instances.

VALSE also allows evaluation of how changes to a facility, for example a hospital waiting room, affect the behaviors of the occupants. If a hospital were to reorganize the furniture in their waiting room, would that have an impact on the way in which users occupy the space? Would the users change the space on their own? How might we use this knowledge to make more useful and comfortable settings?

In addition, there is the possibility of the development of real-time, responsive environments able to interpret behavior and suggest short term or immediately adaptive settings. Imagine an Alzheimer's disease facility that is not just bricks and mortar but is able to track and understand the meaningful behaviors of the patients 24 hours a day, 365 days a year, understanding individual variation in behavior over both the short and the long term. For example, Alzheimer's patients typically have trouble with spatial and visual issues, unable to distinguish between a shadow cast on the floor and a step. Intelligent architectural settings will be able to maintain surveillance and understand the changes in meaningful behavior. This could be a flexible and programmable architectural setting that could become a part of the therapeutic setting, allowing adjustments to individual patient's therapy, creating an improved quality of life for the residents.

VALSE currently exists only in a prototype form; implementation in real-world settings would require extensive development. Additional systems that provide systematic understanding of human movement, location, and meaning seem likely to emerge and offer new ways to engage the human occupation of architecture.

Notes

1 Cited in Samuel, Flora. *Le Corbusier and the Architectural Promenade*. Birkhäuser, 2010.
2 Benjamin, Walter. *The Work of Art in the Age of Mechanical Reproduction*. New York, 1935.
3 "The Extraordinary History of Burning Man". www.farandwide.com. Retrieved June 18, 2020.
4 Holson, Laura M., "How Burning Man Has Evolved Over Three Decades," *New York Times*, August 30, 2018.
5 Debord, Guy. "Theory of the Dérive." *Internationale situationniste* 2.20.05 (1958): 2015.
6 Rohrmeier, K. and Bassett, S., 2015. Planning Burning Man: The Black Rock City Mirage. *The California Geographer* 54, no. 1 (2015): 23–46.
7 "Breathing Spaces: A Pedagogical Exploration of Dance and Architecture" was accepted at the World Dance Alliance-Americas Assembly hosted by the University of Texas at El Paso from February 13–17, 2019.

8 Tufte, Edward R., and Peter R. Graves-Morris. *The visual display of quantitative information. Vol. 2*. Cheshire, CT: Graphics press, 1983.
Tufte, E.R. (1991) "Envisioning information," *Optometry & Vision Science* 68, 4: 322–324.
9 For example, see Nest Thermostat or US patent by Huppi, Brian (19 Nov 2010). "System and method for integrating sensors in thermostats".
10 Lu, Jiakang; Sookoor, Tamim; Srinivasan, Vijay; Gao, Ge; Holben, Brian; Stankovic, John; Field, Eric; Whitehouse, Kamin (2010). "The smart thermostat". *Proceedings of the 8th ACM Conference on Embedded Networked Sensor Systems – Sen Sys '10*. p. 211.
11 Alam, Muhammad Raisul, Mamun Bin Ibne Reaz, and Mohd Alauddin Mohd Ali. "A review of smart homes—Past, present, and future." *IEEE transactions on systems, man, and cybernetics, part C (applications and reviews)* 42, no. 6 (2012): 1190–1203.
12 Solaimani, Sam, Wally Keijzer-Broers, and Harry Bouwman. "What we do–and don't–know about the Smart Home: an analysis of the Smart Home literature." *Indoor and Built Environment* 24, no. 3 (2015): 370–383.
13 Pentland, A., et al. (2005) "Human dynamics: computation for organizations," *Pattern Recognition Letters* 26, 4: 503–511.
14 Waber, B. (2013) *People Analytics: How Social Sensing Technology Will Transform Business and what it Tells Us about the Future of Work*, FT Press.
15 Olguín, D., et al (2009) "Sensible organizations: technology and methodology for automatically measuring organizational behavior," *IEEE Transactions on Systems, Man, and Cybernetics, Part B (Cybernetics)* 39, 1: 43–55.
16 Pentland, A. (2009) "Reality mining of mobile communications: loward a new deal on data," The Global Information Technology Report: 1981.
17 Waber, Ben. *People analytics: How social sensing technology will transform business and what it tells us about the future of work*. FT Press, 2013.
18 Whitehead, Carolyn. "Ten Years of Time Utilisation Studies." AECOM Blog, June 30, 2014. Accessed July 25, 2024. https://aecom.com/blog/ten-years-of-time-utilisation-studies-2/.
19 Williams, Mani, Jane Burry, Asha Rao, and Nathan Williams. "A system for tracking and visualizing social interactions in a collaborative work environment." In *Proceedings of the Symposium on Simulation for Architecture & Urban Design*, pp. 1–4. 2015.
20 Beorkrem, Christopher, Steve Danilowicz, Eric Sauda, Richard Souvenir, Scott Spurlock, and Donna Lanclos. "Keeping an eye out: real time, real world modeling of behavior in health care settings." In *Modelling Behaviour: Design Modelling Symposium* 2015, pp. 459–467. Springer International Publishing, 2015.
21 Spurlock, S. and Souvenir, R. (2012) "Dynamic subset selection for multi-camera tracking," *Proceedings of the 50th Annual Southeast Regional Conference*. ACM. Spurlock, S. and Souvenir, R. (2014) "Multi-view action recognition one camera at a time," *IEEE Winter Conference on Applications of Computer Vision*. IEEE. Spurlock, S., Wu. H., and Souvenir, R. (2014) "Multi-view recognition using weighted view selection," *Asian Conference on Computer Vision*. Springer International Publishing.
22 Churchill, E.F., et al. The Plasma Poster Network: Posting Multimedia Content in Public Places. in *INTERACT*. 2003. McDonald, D.W., et al., Proactive displays: Supporting awareness in fluid social environments. *ACM Transactions on Computer-Human Interaction*, 2008. 14(4): p. 1–31.

23 Connaway, L.S., D. White, and D. Lanclos, Visitors and residents: What motivates engagement with the digital information environment? *Proceedings of the American Society for Information Science and Technology*, 2011. 48(1): p. 1–7. Lanclos, D. and L.S. Connaway. "I find Google a lot easier than going to the library website." Imagine Ways to Innovate and Inspire Students to Use the Academic Library. in *Proceedings of the Association of College & Research Libraries (ACRL)*. 2013. Indianapolis, IN.

24 Heierman, E. and D.J. Cook. Improving Home Automation by Discovering Regularly Occurring Device Usage Patterns. *in Proceedings of the International Conference on Data Mining*. 2003.

7

INFORMATION

Mobile, proxemic, and augmented reality

Ivan Sutherland was a pioneer in computer science who during a long career at MIT, Utah, Caltech, and Berkeley made contributions including the first object-oriented software system, the first fully graphics interface (Sketchpad), and research on 3D computer graphics and printer languages (leading to Adobe software). But in a more poetic mood, he imagined:

> The ultimate display would, of course, be a room within which the computer can control the existence of matter. A chair displayed in such a room would be good enough to sit in. Handcuffs displayed in such a room would be confining, and a bullet displayed in such a room would be fatal. With appropriate programming such a display could literally be the Wonderland into which Alice walked.[1]
>
> (p. 507)

His description of the display and its ability to control matter is far beyond the capabilities available in 1965 (or 2024). But it assumes an explicitly architectural setting (a room) as the native location for such a display and that the display would locate mathematical and physical information in three-dimensional space. That is what we will explore in this chapter.

DOI: 10.4324/9781003363392-7

Mobile interaction

Beginning in 2006, the proliferation of smartphones altered the way humans engage with and encounter their environment. Smartphones are essential components of our daily apparel that weave together information about our location, our activities, and our time. Social media applications are illustrative of this change; in 2013, nearly 500 million messages were sent on Twitter, 80% of them on mobile devices. Social media predates smartphones, but its use and ubiquity has been greatly expanded. As Jordan Frith has noted

> smartphone usage does not represent a simple extension of older internet practices ... Many smartphone applications add an important element to the way people interact with digital information: physical location ... providing users with information about their surroundings.[2]

To provide information about our surroundings, smartphones usually map our position in a two-dimensional space which the phone uses to update our understanding of our surroundings. We rely on applications using positional information including mapping (Google Maps, Waze), gaming apps (Pókemon Go, Zombie Run, Ingress Prime), business crowd-source reviews (Yelp, Tripadvisor), and travel apps (GasBuddy, Uber, Tour Guide). Even applications that are not explicitly about location such as news apps use their knowledge of position to target advertisements and offers.

This has given rise to the field of locative (location-based) media, a virtual medium of communication, functionally bound to a location. Locative media delivers multimedia and other content directly to the user of a mobile device. Jason Farman has developed a theoretical framework in *Mobile Interface Theory: Embodied Space and Locative Media*.[3] Mobile technologies are transforming everyday life, allowing users to connect and interact with the internet while moving through a variety of locations. This creates an embodied identity that results from the interweaving of virtual and material space.

Our relative position to other objects in our surroundings, interpreted through a map, is a familiar experience. Before smartphones, this information would be embedded in spaces in static maps and signage. Anyone who has been to a mall or a subway station might have seen wayfinding maps showing a "You Are Here" point. Our relative position in our surroundings is only one of the many information points that we interpret as we move about in space. Colors, names, landmarks, and types of activities are all parts of the dynamic set of information that we use to understand our surroundings. Architects, through their design, influence this information space.

Architecture and information

Historically, architects have tried to connect buildings with information, meanings, rituals, and activities that take place within them. This connection sometimes occurs through explicit embedding of information in the space, and at other times through the meaningful organization of elements within the space or associating symbolic elements to their designs.

One example is the tympanum of Vézelay Abbey in Burgundy, completed in the 1130s. Literacy rates ranging from 7 to 18% have been estimated for this period; the tympanum is intended to illustrate the teaching of the church for those who could not read the Bible directly. The tympanum was "a visualization of both the Pentecost and a passage from the book of Ephesians chapter 2."[4] Vestigial sculptural programs such as the "stations of the cross" remain present in Roman Catholic churches, although they are given much less prominence.

Anagogy is central to Gothic architecture, where the visible constantly refers to what is invisible but intelligible.[5] The builders of these structures intimate that something can actually be experienced and known of the unseen. According to arguably the first Gothic architect, Abbot Suger of Saint Denis, every aspect of the new apse architecture had a symbolic meaning. The 12 columns separating the chapels, he wrote, represented the 12 Apostles.[6]

The English gardens at Stourhead laid out from 1741 to 1780 are another example of reference to exterior texts indexed to design. The lake at Stourhead is artificially created following a path around the lake and is meant to evoke a journey similar to that of Aeneas' descent into the underworld.[7] Passages telling of Aeneas's journey are quoted in the temples surrounding the lake. Monuments are used to frame one another; for example the Pantheon designed by Flitcroft entices the visitor over, but once reached, views from the opposite shore of the lake beckon. Understanding the gardens relied on the classical education at Oxford and Cambridge shared by the gentlemen visitors, which included reading Homer's *Iliad* in Greek.

Amazon fulfillment warehouses, the largest of which is 3.8 million square feet, have arrived at a different intersection of information and space, where the spatial organization is dependent on data.[8] Typical warehouses are sorted in fixed spatial locations by item, type, or manufacturer, with all identical items located together. Amazon has adopted random location storage products that are stored in any available location, rather than being assigned to specific predetermined locations. The database keeps track in real time of each of the millions of items in the warehouse. Advances in database management and wireless communication have connected all workers, machine, or human, to all the millions of items and their locations, minimizing the distances needed to complete an order. Some work has been done on using Google Glass augmented reality in this setting.[9] Space and information have been woven together into a tight, shifting fabric.

A proposal for a new Los Angeles County Art Museum by the Office of Metropolitan Architecture is a radical approach to the design of a museum proposing multiple interpretations. Rather than a series of galleries arranged in chronological order or by country or culture where space and information are coerced to fit one narrative, Koolhaas imagines the freedom to explore many. This proposal provides an open floor of art under a single large-scale roof that can be explored through a large variety of pathways. As Koolhaas says, "Imagine an almost utopian condition where the history … told as a simultaneous narrative showing coincidence, autonomy, influence, and convergence."[10] This proposal treats the collections as a whole, instead of a series of galleries. It allows multiple paths, interpretations, and cross-curatorial exhibits.

Human–computer interaction (HCI) into space

HCI research has also become interested in the relationship between location and information.

Ubiquitous computing (Ubicomp) is a concept that emerged at Palo Alto Research Center (PARC) in the 1980s and 1990s. The leading advocate at PARC was Mark Weiser, who published the seminal definition in 1993.[11] As a contrast to the dominant paradigm of the desktop computer, he imagines an environment where the computer is present anytime and everywhere and becomes invisible. Several critical technical innovations made the coordination of these devices possible: the miniaturization of computing and display hardware and the development of communication technology (Wi-Fi, Bluetooth) to knit the devices together and allow them to seamlessly share data. Originally these devices were seen as existing at three scales: tabs, pads, and board (which we might now identify perhaps as phone, tablet, and wall monitor). As Ubicomp has developed, the number and kind of devices has proliferated. Cars, refrigerators, thermostats, speakers, heaters, televisions, and air conditioners are a small sample of smart devices that are present in virtually every environment. And possible future devices have been suggested including: dust, micro-electro-mechanical systems micrometers to millimeters in size; skin: flexible non-planar display surfaces as clothes and curtains; and paint: nano-devices painted onto surfaces forming a network.[12] The distinction between a computer as an object and its spatial context is at least blurred and likely irrelevant.

In addition, research on eye tracking and gaze detection has been implemented for desktop systems[13] and more recently for headset based systems that connect information display locations and content including most recently Apple Vision Pro. More sophisticated work by Saul Greenberg on proxemic interaction[14] begins with insights from the anthropologist Edward Hall that identifies four proxemic zones guiding interpersonal interaction ranging from intimate to personal to social to public.[15] Each zone brings with it expectations of the scope and nature of informational exchange; a computer system should change what it displays based on the movement and position of the humans within the space. Detailed text presentation may be well suited to those close to a screen, while a graphic format may be better for those engaged at a greater distance. A proxemic interface should include awareness of distance, orientation, movement, identity, and location. As William Buxton observed, "When you walk up to your computer ... does it even know if you are there? ... a motion-sensing light switch is 'smarter' than any of the switches in the computer."[16]

Based on this premise, Greenberg developed a proxemic toolkit (see Figure 7.1) that can be used to create a wide range of proxemic interactions that tracks objects and their proximity relationship, generating highly accurate information as a series of easy to program events.[17] Programming in this toolkit is simple enough to be used by students with brief training to construct interesting proximity-aware applications. This creation of toolkits is a common feature of HCI research, allowing easy access to existing techniques that can be used to design new interactions. The toolkit has been used to create context-aware media players and proxemic game players. This approach works best to connect computers to an extended understanding of context, but the lack of a systematic structure of architectural space limits this attempt for entire buildings, campuses, or environments.

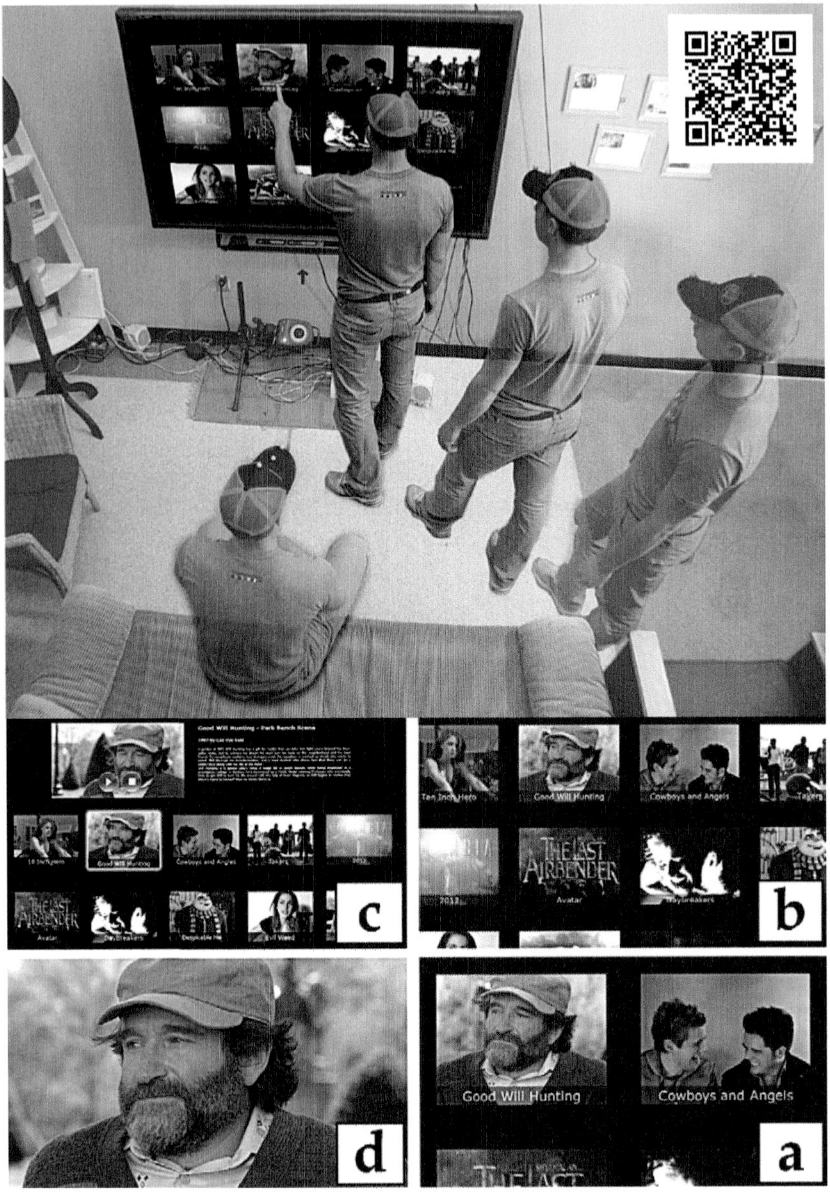

FIGURE 7.1 Proxemic interaction: (a) activating the system when a person enters the room, (b) continuously revealing more content with decreasing distance of the person to the display, (c) allowing explicit interaction through direct touch when person is at close distance, and (d) implicitly switching to full screen view when person is taking a seat. Image courtesy of Saul Greenberg, Nicolai Marquardt, Till Ballendat, Rob Diaz-Marino; reprinted with permission.

Augmented reality

We have seen that architects and designers have embedded information in space to enable human understanding. Contemporary developments in HCI have expanded the possibilities for how information might be presented to people as they move through the world. These possibilities include connecting people wirelessly to large data sources, aligning visual information to the perspective view of people, and customizing what information to display for people's interest. Considerable progress has been made, making it possible to imagine augmented reality (AR) as a fluid media rather than a science experiment.

Presenting user interfaces in space while keeping track of their location has been a challenging problem. The earliest AR systems were designed to operate using simple sensing devices and projectors. The sensors would trigger a projector to display relevant information on the wall and change the information as users shifted locations. If we want to go beyond locating a person and also situate virtual objects and information in a person's real world, we are faced with more difficult challenges. Not only do we need to keep track of the location of the user, but we also need to have the means to scan and track objects in the physical world and update the information accordingly; such interfaces are fully deserving of the name AR. Although the majority of advancements in AR are around presenting visual information on top of the real world, it can also include auditory or haptic elements. In fact, some of the earliest works in AR, such as Virtual Fixtures developed by Louis Rosenberg in 1992, incorporated manipulating physical objects that would be reflected in a 3D virtual world.

Ever since the early conception of AR ideas, there have been numerous advancements. In the 2000s, ARToolkit was released which made it easier for developers to use computer vision to create AR applications that align virtual objects in the real world. In 2009, smartphones made enough advancements that enabled ARToolkit to work on mobile devices. In the 2010s, AR technology was greatly improved. Google Glass was released, and although it did not prove popular with consumers for privacy reasons, it showed the great potential of wearables. In 2014, Microsoft introduced Hololens, a self-contained computer in a head-mounted display. Packing amazing computing power in a relatively small device, Hololens was able to project high-quality virtual objects in the real world while allowing users to interact with them.

It was in 2016 that AR applications had their biggest boom. Designed for smartphones, Niantic released Pókemon Go. Using simple smartphone interactions, Pókemon Go leveraged the smartphone camera and enabled players to interact with virtual Pókemon in different parts of a city. The AR system was simple: a player would point a camera at a location shown on a map and would see a virtual Pókemon. By clicking on the smartphone, the player would capture the virtual character. The game became a cultural phenomenon and at its peak had millions playing, using AR through smartphones.

In AR, interaction techniques are also unique and an important challenge in interface design. As already discussed, for mobile AR systems like Pókemon Go, interaction is done through touch, just like other smartphone apps. For more immersive AR systems like Hololens, we have seen many innovations in embodied interactions. Hololens, for example, enabled users to point at an object and, with a simple gesture, interact with virtual objects. Other systems also provide dedicated physical controllers that provide finer controls to users.

More recently, in 2024 we have seen interaction techniques to be much more natural. With the advancements of AI, conversational interactions through voice have become much more streamlined. Most recent mixed reality devices, including Meta's smart glasses that only interact through voice, have implemented impressive conversational interactions powered by large language models.

Vision Pro, Apple's foray into what it calls "spatial interfaces," has made major advancements in consumer-ready embodied interactions. The device uses internal cameras to track eye movement, by combining gaze with hand flick gestures to interact with User Interface (UI) elements situated in the physical world. The gaze interactions for Apple's AR device are among the best and most natural to use. One famous technology YouTube commentator, MKBHD, who has millions of followers, called the interaction "borderline telepathic." Interaction technologies are likely to become more and more natural.

AR experiences are designed to adapt at a very simple level to any spatial setting. However, in most current applications, the nature of the space and the activities within it remain underdeveloped. The potential of designing AR applications and architectural settings together can allow for the exploration of a full range of affordances, feedback mechanisms, and output/display options. AR can exemplify embodied interaction and address the historical overemphasis on symbolic systems.[18] An understanding of architectural space and place is not circumstantial, but rather essential to how interaction can be meaningful to users.

Vision Pro, Apple's latest break into AR applications, is a technological marvel. However, looking at the promotional videos, we see a lot of isolated individuals sitting on a couch, individually watching videos on large AR screens. Mrwhosetheboss, a tech YouTuber who was present in the room where Vision Pro was announced, delivered the following review:[19]

> I do think this is the start of the end of shared experiences. At the end of the apple event, where they were leading up to announcing the price, they were like if you bought a massive TV and a proper sound system, you'd spend like 12k, but with this, all of those things together are just 3.5 thousand. But the key thing missing from that is that a cinema room is an experience for a family. This is an experience for one. I mean yeah you could buy four or five for a family, and technically watch the same film all at once, but what I imagine is a more likely scenario where everyone is just watching their own thing. And that core human connection that we discovered when we discovered fire would start to fade.

Although we don't share the same predictions for changes in human activities as Mrwhosetheboss, he does raise a key point here. The design of the existing Vision Pro has not considered the current way that people want to watch movies together. This need, the meaning behind a "cinema room," could be part of the design of the AR application. And AR designers, through a process of ethnography, could have come to a clearer understanding of human behavior that drives potential usages of AR.

Recall that the activities in Pókemon Go are designed around points of interest in different cities. In a sense, then, this game is an AR application with some integration into human activities. But is it designed considering the population dynamics of the city? Dr. Kishonna Gray's keynote speech at the ACM Conference on Human Factors in Computing Systems (CHI) 2022 in New Orleans about Pókemon Go activities in Chicago stated that:[20,21]

> I'm like no matter where we are we can do Pókemon Go. ... I couldn't have been more wrong! When we went out there trying to find the pokey ... there were none around! There was one! It was a sad statue in the park and it was a Confederate statue.

This story conveys that it is not sufficient to consider a shallow notion of activity and disregard the underlying social dynamics. Even though activities in Pókemon Go are designed around points where activities already occur, it is then inevitable that the injustices already present in the city are reflected in the information and activities in the AR game. Through a more in-depth integration with urban dynamics, we might be able to create new virtual spaces that do not reinforce and reflect the same dynamics that exist in our spaces.

Research in AR specifically within the architecture communities has similarly neglected such concerns. While active research has been conducted on AR and virtual reality (VR) in computer science since the 1970s,[22] the interest in the use of AR in architecture has focused primarily on applications during design, construction, and post-occupancy. Technologies including GPS, cloud computing, and mobile computing are potentially important ways of advancing the construction process, exploring various aspects including design collaboration, construction, visualization, and education.[23] Head-mounted AR systems can be used during the architecture renovation process[24] as well as to visualize designs, modifications, and extensions to a building in an outdoor environment.[25] Research on the use of AR technology in learning situations applicable to architecture focuses on general principles including gamification and curiosity as well as superior spatial understanding using interactive 3D AR models versus printed plans.[26]

Work from media studies situates AR in a broader cultural and historical context.[27] Any understanding of the use of AR must include how it compares with existing methods of engagement. Mnemosyne is a system that delivers a personalized, interactive, multimedia experience to museum visitors through the use of computer vision.[28] Although AR will differ technologically, the issue of personalization is central to its use.[29] The Transformative Museum project is an important framework for this understanding in a broad context.

The development of AR applications in architectural and urban settings has increased with these expanded technical capabilities. Earlier attempts to embed AR into architectural and urban environments[30] anticipated salient elements of the Hololens system but in a form requiring cumbersome hardware.

Unlike VR which replaces the real world with a three-dimensional simulation, AR combines the real world and computer-generated content. Great effort has been expended on accurate registration of the virtual and real objects. The release of advanced AR devices has introduced new, interactive, hybrid spaces infused and organized with information. Space is the natural setting for AR, suggesting the possibility of an architectural interface. In computer science, this spatial setting is often ignored except for issues of registration.

Augmented reality into architecture

It is essential to design AR applications with an understanding of the spatial and ethnographic context. A thick description is needed, not just sensors that map the surfaces accurately in the proximity of our headset, but one that is based on the physical environment created by spatial design and the human activities by those who occupy it and give it meaning. To explore this challenge, we created a series of design sessions in collaboration with experts from HCI and ethnography. These sessions focused on embedding AR applications at an existing museum in Charlotte, North Carolina. The Bechtler Museum of Modern Art in Charlotte North Carolina (see Error! Reference source not found.) is a relatively small museum exhibiting modern paintings and sculptures. The museum entrance leads to a spacious lobby that often features installations and smaller exhibits. At the moment, a rendition of a Sol Lewitt wall artwork is visible as visitors enter. The galleries and exhibition spaces are spread over four floors with several galleries of different sizes. Some galleries are connected to outdoor spaces such as terraces that also showcase art pieces and sculptures. The museum also includes areas dedicated to educational events and accommodates workshops, lectures, and multimedia exhibits.

One important function of a museum is to present artifacts that the public is interested in viewing. In the case of Bechtler and other art museums, the artifacts are paintings and sculptures. In the case of a science museum such as Chicago's Field Museum, the artifacts are archeological pieces. Although the types of artifacts vary, all museums need to present information to visitors. The information is usually presented in the form of wall graphics. In our first exploration of AR, we assumed that there is a great deal of information that might be interesting to visitors but that the amount is limited by the extent of physical space and the need to keep the focus on the artifacts themselves. The challenge was to design applications that allow museum curators to present deeper and more dynamic information using AR.

We started by surveying how information about art pieces is presented in the museum and how visitors see them. We identified two main information types that were integrated into the architecture of the museum:

FIGURE 7.2 Bechtler Museum of Modern Art, Charlotte, North Carolina. Image courtesy of Konstantinos Koukopoulos.

information about each artifact and information about exhibitions and collections of artifacts.

The most prevalent type of information presentation was about each artifact, presented as graphics attached adjacently to each piece. From the placement and design of the graphics, it was clear that the curators aimed to put the primary focus on art pieces. We observed that visitors viewed artifacts from relatively far distances (i.e. 10–20 feet). However, the information graphics were smaller and unobtrusive. In the example of Figure 7.3, the graphics include a picture and the name of the artist in large font accompanied by the location base of the artist as a subtitle. The artist information is followed by the name of the piece, materials, and methods used to create it. The information is followed by a few paragraphs about the art piece written in smaller font. Aside from the name of the artist and the artifact, the rest of the information needs to be read very close (1–2 feet) to the information.

In addition to information about each artifact, each collection, usually contained within a room, is identified by the name of the collection, the artists involved, and a paragraph about included arts and artists. These graphics were usually larger in size, and placed strategically so that visitors are exposed to the overview before viewing the individual pieces of art.

Looking closely, other types of information were embedded within the space as well. Signage that helps visitors navigate the museum and find their collections of interest or a specific artwork was the other primary type of information that was not directly related to individual pieces. This information was also presented through pamphlets that included maps and other useful information for visitors.

In virtually all museums, the information accompanied by the artifacts is curated by a group of experts who are in charge of providing it to visitors. Having learned about the different kinds of information integrated into different spaces at Bechtler, an interview with the lead curator elicited their goals and challenges in designing information for visitors. Several salient themes came out of our interview:

- **Layers of information** suggest presentations should include information at different levels of depth and categories, including information about the artist's life and career, the materials and techniques used, and the history of the piece.
- **Storytelling and context** highlight the importance of telling the stories behind the art and putting it in context. This includes the artist's body of work, the history of the piece, and the larger artistic movement it's a part of. Digital tools are a way to overcome physical limitations and provide this context effectively.

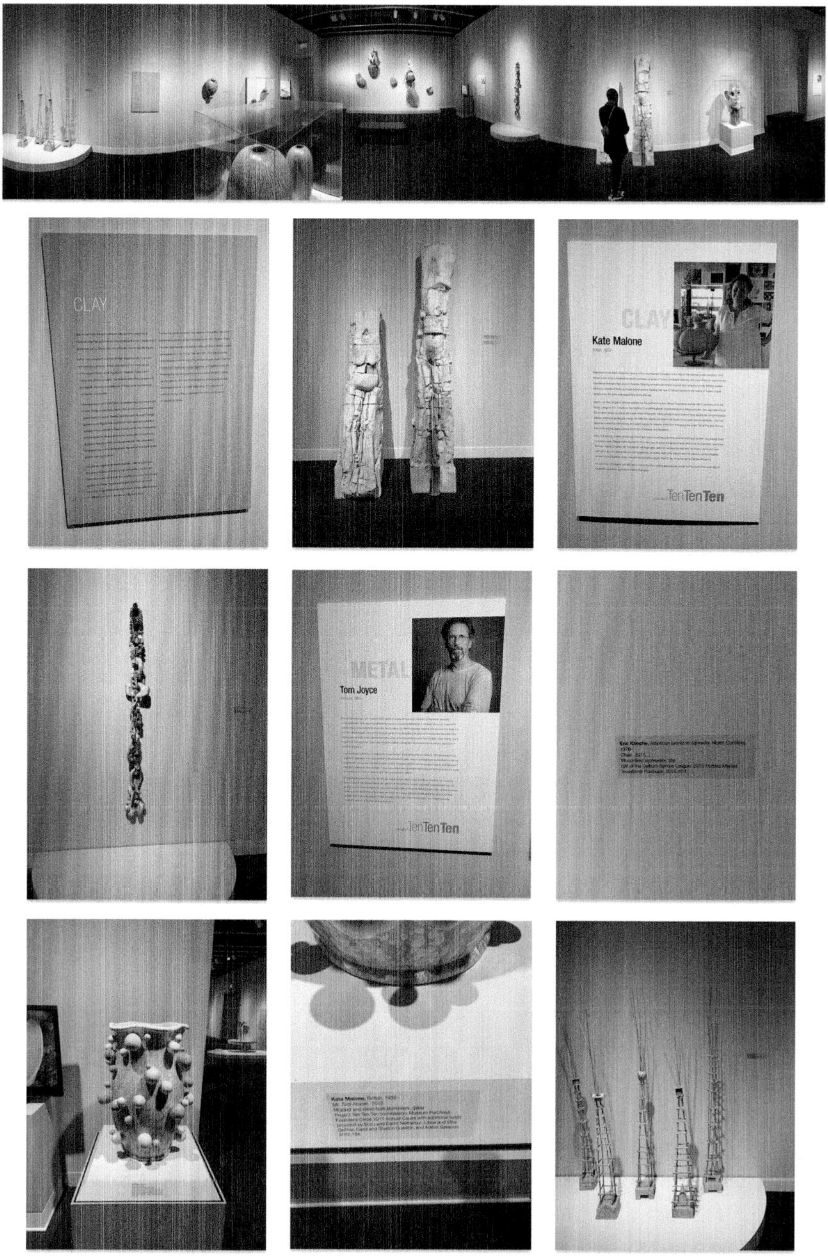

FIGURE 7.3 Different types of information presented in museums as signage.

- **Forms of information** suggest presenting the information in a variety of formats for improving engagement including audio, video, and manipulable images, to cater to diverse learning styles and interests. This would allow visitors to explore art in a more interactive and engaging way.
- **Accessibility and personalization** might involve using digital tools to provide layered information and personalized experiences, allowing visitors to explore their own interests within the collection. An example of such personalized tools is apps or dedicated audio narration devices used in museums.
- **Challenges of limited space and physical restrictions** are a concern for most museums. Using digital technology could provide information about artwork that's not on display or to offer alternative perspectives on individual pieces.

As described by the curator, different categories of information are already presented in varying levels of detail. The existing static designs enable this through varying font sizes that are legible by moving closer to the sign. To explore how an interactive and dynamic AR application might improve the ability to meet the design, an evaluation of an AR prototype was developed in 2017 for the Bechtler Museum.

Implementation of this prototype was fairly straightforward. A 3D sculpture was used as an artifact. To overlay dynamic information on real objects, an AR app needs to somehow detect those objects. Today, many advanced technologies exist and newer hardware is well suited to this task. At the time, we used existing image detection technology to detect the sculpture using the Hololens headset. Detecting the artifact provides us with a point in virtual space. All modern AR hardware can easily maintain the position of a point (in this case, the artifact) in relation to the headset as a user is moving around. Using this information allowed a calculation of the distance between the visitor (the position of the headset) and the artifact (the detected sculpture). Using this information we can map different levels of detail to distance, and different categories of information to a user's orientation while displaying virtual information that orthogonally faces the user as they move through the space.

We designed four levels of information into thresholds of distances (see Figure 7.4). For example, at the farthest distance of more than 30 feet, the visitor sees the name of the artifact in a large font. As they move closer to the artifact, more information is shown. The closest distance of less than 15 feet, a paragraph with a small but legible font is displayed, for visitors to learn the most amount of information about the artifact.

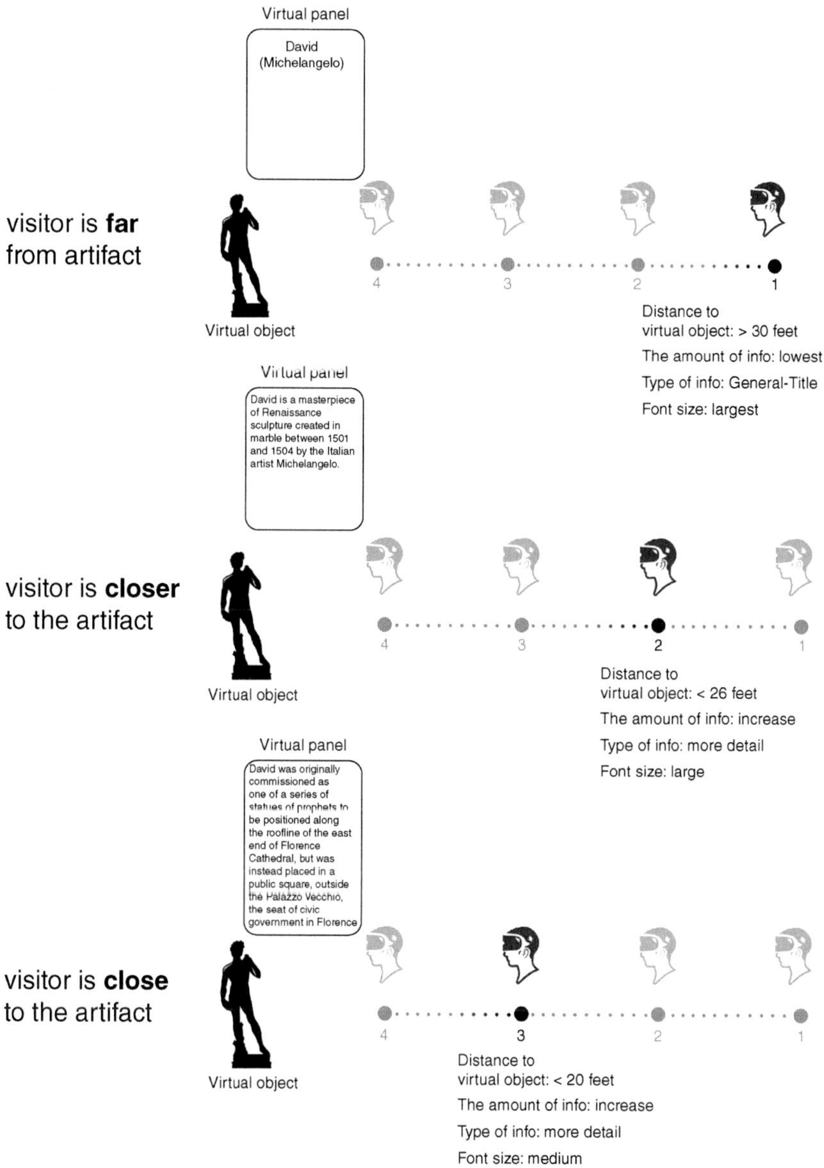

FIGURE 7.4 Augmented reality experiments to provide dynamic information about museum artifacts. Image courtesy of Alireza Fatemi.

We also learned that different categories of information are presented to visitors including the artist, the art piece and methods used to create it, and the historical context of the art. However, the physical space of the signage limits the amount of detail that can be presented to visitors simultaneously. In AR, however, we can overcome this information by dynamically changing the information category based on users' positions. One obvious factor would be how close or far a viewer is from the object which might display information about the artifact itself in less or greater detail. A second factor might be the angle of the viewer relative to the object, directly in front or the artifact or at an angle from the left or right. If they are looking from the right of the artifact, they might see a second category of information such as the historical context, including the artist, and if they are looking from the left, they can see a third category, such as the materials and methods used to create it.

Using distance thresholds as a trigger for different levels of detail and orientation towards the object as a trigger for different categories of information, we arrived at nine zones of information for presenting dynamic information based on visitors' movement and position and relation to each artifact. We conducted a user study with two artifacts, a sculpture and wall art, with 11 participants who provided us with a recording of visitors' think-aloud as they explored information about artifacts in AR and a Point of View (POV) video for each participant. Using the POV video, we were able to study how visitors move around the objects to explore the provided information, and from think-aloud, we collected initial feedback about challenges we might face in developing such applications for museums.

Let us consider the movement patterns of one participant (Figure 7.5 top) based on the POV footage we collected. We can clearly see that this participant moved around and explored the dynamic information from various angles and distances. But we can also see that the participant was moving back and forth between different levels of detail several times. This means that at least some of the movement is users simply learning about and familiarizing themselves with seeing different levels of details based on distance. Although (Figure 7.5 bottom) looks like a bowl of spaghetti, we see that denser areas of movement around thresholds which shows this is a common pattern of behavior among participants.

Instead, let's now consider when visitors pause during their movement. In (Figure 7.5 middle) the points show the stopping points of all visitors. We see very few stop points in the farthest zones that show the least amount of detail which is expected because reading one simple sentence in large font does not really require stopping. We do, however, see much more stopping points in the zones that provide more detail in front of the artifacts. This suggests that participants are likely to gradually get comfortable

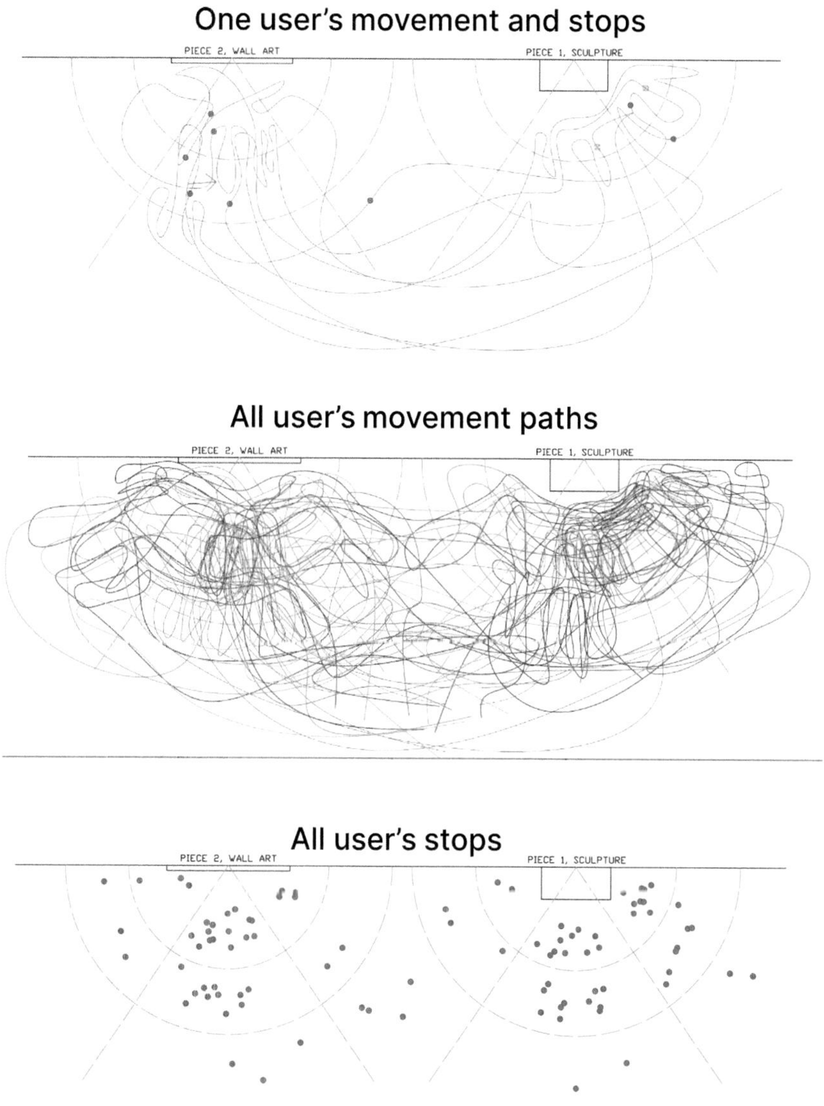

FIGURE 7.5 Visuals showing users' movements and pauses during user study sessions in the Bechtler Museum. Image courtesy of Alireza Fatemi.

with distance as a trigger for viewing different levels of detail and use the feature as they naturally view artifacts.

Although we do observe movement to the right and left side of the artifacts as visitors learn about the different categories, we see much fewer stopping points in the right and left zones. Asking the participants after using the application revealed that, indeed, visitors find it much more natural and simpler to look at the artifacts from the front side. If we were to design this interface to this behavior pattern, we might need to try new strategies that allow visitors to change the categories of information at will without having to change orientations.

AR applications can go beyond replacing existing information in spaces with more dynamic ones. As experiencing a museum is often a social experience where groups of people visit together, and interact with artifacts, we can design more social applications. We can imagine applications that allow visitors to communicate interesting nuggets of information for others to experience. Such applications have already been tried in another, surprisingly related domain of video games.

Many video games encourage people to hangout and socially interact in virtual spaces. For AR, one of the most interesting applications of sharing information comes from Dark Souls, a very difficult game with a dedicated community of players. The goal in Dark Souls is to use swords to slay very strong monsters (nothing new). Instead of providing heavy tutorials that take away from immersion within the game, a social feature allows the community to help each other by leaving information as points for others to see. If a lost warrior is trying to figure out what to do next, they might see a blinking icon permanently placed on the ground. Interacting with the point reveals a message left by another player; the game also allows players to like or dislike the messages. And the information that is most liked, is more likely to remain in the space permanently. This feature could be adapted to leave spatially located information in the context of museums. Museum visitors could leave a message as a 3D object in space. Other visitors can see the message and if they find it useful, they can interact with the like button. The application can use the social interactions such as like or dislike to filter through and show more relevant spatialized bits of information to visitors. A prototype of this application has been designed but awaits testing. How do we incentivize leaving information? How can we prevent malicious information? How can we differentiate information left by curators from ones left by the public?

Augmented reality/architecture hybrid design process[31]

AR is designed for existing buildings, aided by scanning technology to locate adjacent surfaces. But designing architecture that is tightly integrated with AR offers the possibility for architectural elements that can have a powerful role in the unfolding experience of the building with an expanded understanding of the assembled knowledge supporting it. This means that architects must engage the dynamic nature of human occupation. To achieve this goal, a model for a hybrid AR/architectural design process is required. This process is based in part on work by the philosopher Donald Schön's whose theory of reflective practice is associated with the experience of surprise. Schön suggests that, by "reflecting-in-action," professionals reflect on unexpected experiences and conduct "experiments" which serve to generate both a new understanding of the experience and a change in the situation.[32] Multiple designs can serve to uncover an expanded range of possibilities. As Schön describes in a detailed examination of an architectural studio:

> Architecture is a profession rooted in the artistry of designing, a process I have characterized as a special form of reflection-in-action: reflective conversation with the materials of the design situation. In this sense, I suggest, architecture embodies a kind of artistry that is also sometimes practiced in other professions, especially in the indeterminate zones of practice. It is through variants on the process of reflection-in-action that competent practitioners sometimes deal well with uncertainty, uniqueness, and value-conflict.[33]
>
> (p. 9)

From an HCI perspective, Mary Lou Maher has proposed that evolution can be a useful metaphor to describe this design process. Given the changes to a problem and possible solutions that occur during the design process, she introduces the concept of co-evolutionary design: a system that can generate and recognize emergent structure and behavior.[34]

To explore this idea, the Mount Zion Archaeological Park in Jerusalem, the site of archaeological excavations close to completion, is ideal. The design of a museum and park preserving and explaining the archeological and cultural artifacts found within the site presents challenges both architecturally and for the integration of very large data archives.[35] Huge amounts of data have been generated during the eight years of the excavation (object, location, time) and can be connected to the larger archaeological record across the Middle East and the world. A team of twelve architectural designers, three computational designers, and faculty from departments of architecture, archeology, and computer science engaged in the process of designing tightly coupled AR interactions and architectural spaces in the context of a museum.

This necessitated the creation of a hybrid design process combining user interaction and architectural design. Next, novel tools were developed that explore architectural space using traditional orthographic views combined with real-time interaction. This led to a range of designs for an interactive archeology museum that combined 3D AR interactions and space. An outcome of this work was a taxonomy of possible AR interactions in architectural space.

Beginning development separated the architectural space from the AR interaction design. The architectural designers developed schematic designs for the museum as well as ideas about AR interactions. At first the AR interactions were decoupled from the proposed spaces. However, designing architectural space that takes full advantage of AR requires a process that is different from either architecture or interaction design alone. To address this issue, precedent studies of AR technology, archeological museums, and the rare examples of AR integration into architecture were researched. Using these precedent studies, a list of potential AR interactions were developed.

Integrating AR was challenging for architects who are entirely trained in form-based, static space and have little or no experience in interaction design. To rectify this problem, various prototyping and diagramming methods from HCI were combined with the architectural design process. This required an iterative process of architecture and interaction design. As the architectural designers made progress in developing spaces and programs for the museum, they also developed scenarios for reinventing the ways archeological information could be embedded using AR.

The architectural designs were evaluated using normative architectural evaluation methods (static categories including geometry, circulation, views, lighting, and enclosure). Evaluating interactions was more challenging as it required shifting views over time or multiple users. In the beginning, students represented AR interactions with standard HCI mediums such as storyboards, then generating spatial diagrams to situate AR interaction within architectural spaces (the analog step). Next, storytelling was used by the designers to conceptualize architecture/AR synthesis. An interactive desktop application prototype allows simultaneous exploration of architectural design and AR interactions (the digital step). Similar to a video game, our interactive prototype enables designers to navigate 3D spaces while experiencing and interacting with potential AR features.

At the beginning of the design process, after a quick brief about the scope of the course, students were asked to familiarize themselves with AR interactions. Through a few sessions, they also got hands-on (or in this case, heads-on) experience with Microsoft Hololens, a head-mounted display specifically designed for AR interactions.

Architects started by brainstorming the integration of AR within their architecture as they developed their designs. Each designer developed diagrams and models creating fulsome descriptions of their proposed AR integrations and storyboards attempting to combine AR with space, either by hand sketching or using familiar sketching software. However, it was difficult for the designers to imagine AR interactions in a spatial setting, and the proposed solutions were not fully developed. Moreover, these storyboards proved to be more useful in communicating innovations but they lacked detailed spatial information.

To enhance how AR ideas are designed in a spatial setting, a "spatial storyboard" technique was developed which consists of schematic maps that are accompanied by flow charts of interactions linked to space (see Figure 7.6). This attempt proved to be more useful for the students. By thinking about space and interactions within a unified representation, the students had the opportunity to iterate and understand their spatial AR designs that fit with their individual rendition of an archeological museum.

Still, a big challenge for the designers was the gap between low-fidelity prototypes of AR interactions embedded with space, and how those interactions would play in a real AR space.

A preliminary list of different categories of interactions could be shared between all designers. The computational designers then developed sample interactions for the Hololens based on the proposals made by architectural designers. Testing with the Hololens proved helpful for architectural designers to better understand the role of AR in their designs. However, there was still a large gap between what architects envisioned for their buildings and how AR would integrate within it. More specifically, it was impossible to show the building model as part of the AR experience. An interface that enables users to explore proposals enables us to import 3D models of buildings and create a walkthrough in the proposed space, as well as to embed the proposed interactions (see Figure 7.7). This system allows users to view the space in both perspective and top view which are conventional architecture representations and interact with proposed AR objects and information, similar to a video game. It also consists of complementary views that show a user's interaction log as well as a view highlighting different AR interactions as a user experiences a proposed intersection of AR and architectural space. This interface allows explorations of proposed museum design and evaluation of its potential as an interface. It also allowed the generation of videos that demonstrated simultaneously both the architectural space and the interactions to help with heuristic evaluations.

The architectural program included preservation of the archeological excavation, a gallery featuring selected artifacts from the site, an extensive archive of artifacts discovered on the site, and a suite of offices and research laboratories for research.

Beginning with the same requirements and site, architectural designers produced a range of different spaces with embedded AR. However, there were wide variations. One project describes the proposed building as

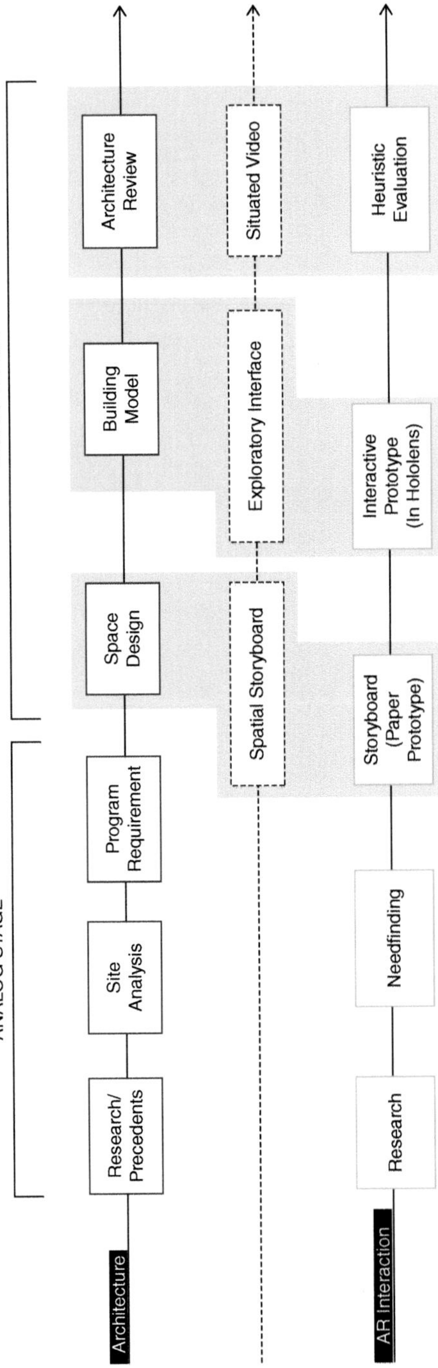

FIGURE 7.6 Hybrid design process for architecture and AR.

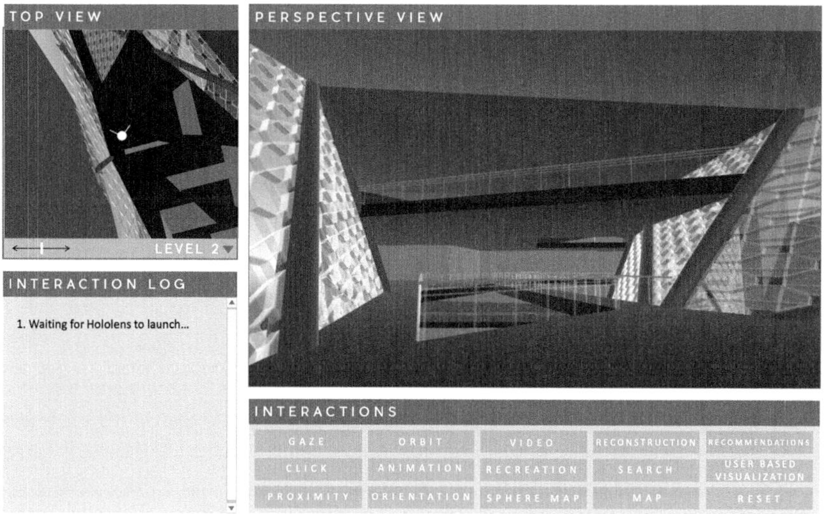

FIGURE 7.7 Game engine based application allowing architects to represent space and AR interactions to stakeholders.

> a pathway around the dig site. The artifacts are displayed in a linear gallery. When the users have the Hololens on, their proximity to the artifacts results in different levels of overview/detailed information being presented about the artifact, and the related location will be highlighted in the dig site.

This work presents information based on proximity of users to each physical object, a feature employed by many architectural designers.

With the goal of exposing the context of the artifacts to the users, another designer chose to include virtual landscape spaces from different eras in proximity to physical artifacts in the galleries. Furthermore, as users explore the dig site, AR reconstructions of structures that existed over time are revealed: the building includes two masses standing on each side of the archaeological dig in order to maintain a visual connection with the dig. The Hololens primarily is being used to display text on artifacts, recreations of artifacts, and virtual objects recreating historical buildings in their specific location on site, and virtual landscape spaces of Jerusalem throughout historical time periods. Not all designers chose to overlay text on physical artifacts. Through fusing data visualization with a central dome, one designer used a gaze target as a means of interacting with a point cloud visualization. She describes the users' experience:

> Users will enter a domed space, where they will interact with a point cloud that represents the quantity of data in the site. The point cloud is color coded by era, to help the user understand and handle the amount

> of information. The interaction starts by detecting the target of one's gaze. As the gaze duration lingers on a point in space, the display expands and virtual objects and text are presented. X-ray views to important city sites occur at the end of each corridor.

A number of designers used AR to display personalized wayfinding throughout their buildings. One proposes using voice input from multiple users to create a curated shared experience by including virtual walls to guide users in a gallery:

> Most of the AR experience happens in a rectangular gallery space. The unique interaction is a shared experience of the users through multiple voices. Based on analysis of these voices, a navigation path will be highlighted with virtual walls, filling the space with desired artifacts. In this approach, the technology allows for a dynamic experience that is shaped through the dialog between visitors as well as interaction with the objects. The virtual objects organize the collection into a virtual space based on the visitors' dialogues.

Another designer proposed a pathway over the dig site, connecting gallery space to the archive located on opposite sides of the site, combining text in the gallery with virtual objects in the dig site:

> In the gallery space, the artifacts are displayed on pedestals. Based on the user's proximity, text is displayed and similar virtual objects will appear in the same space. As the visitor proceeds over the dig site, the virtual objects that float above the pathway will move into place of the exact location they were found, based on the angle of view on the pathway. Physical computing is activated in the archives, opening drawers/cabinets that match a user's interests.

Designers also proposed usage of AR to construct dynamic virtual spaces that allow a group's experience to change based on users' preferences or searches (see Figure 7.8): The building rises from the dig site, surrounded by gallery spaces in upper levels, creating relationships between the two spaces. In the gallery space text will offer the visitors information about the artifacts they view, based on proximity and user preferences. The user can use hand gestures to search based on the era, type and value of the artifacts. This will result in virtual partitions that group artifacts together to direct visitors to their desired search results. In turn, the gallery's virtual space becomes a dynamic component in the museum experience, creating a continually evolving experience.

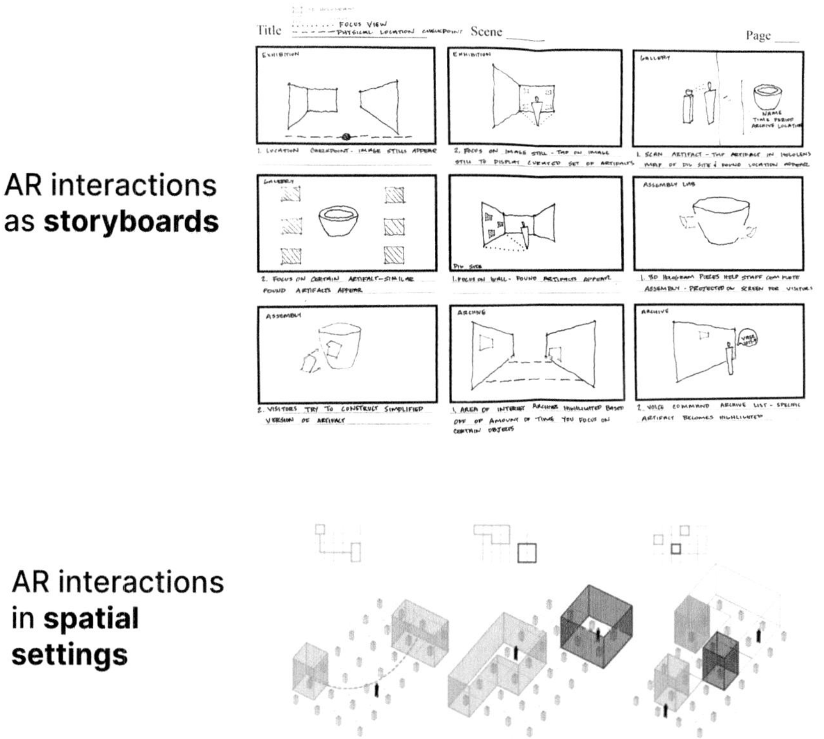

FIGURE 7.8 An example of design proposals by architectural designers.

A wide variety of interaction techniques emerges from these studies leading to a set of connections between the architecture interface and AR compiled into a preliminary taxonomy of possibilities for inputs and outputs.

Interaction types range from direct interactions where users have to activate certain AR views, others include indirect interactions where users' bodies and positions change the AR outputs they see:

- Proximity (indirect): moving close to or further away alters data display.
- Gaze target (indirect): direction is immediately understood.
- Gaze duration (direct): understood after brief use.
- Orientation (indirect): inside/outside or Cartesian direction is understood if architecturally reinforced.
- View direction (indirect): head motion vertically or horizontally is grasped after brief use.

- Hand gesture (direct): using hands to select or move AR objects. This interaction is not naturally afforded, understanding requires significant feedback.
- Voice direction: improving but still error prone requiring significant feedback.

The outputs of the architectural AR system are directly linked to the interaction techniques and can assume either display of physical aspects:

- Physical computing: rearrangement of physical objects based on AR interactions.
- Overview/detail: details made to appear to come closer to user and be available for inspection.
- Transparent/opaque: virtual walls can be selectively closed and opened.
- X-ray vision: allows users to see into adjacent spaces, overlays videos and animations on physical objects.
- Virtual space: generated user moves through space, guiding or circumscribing.
- Heat map: shows the locations of classes of objects.
- Cognitive maps: capture individual interest and present paths through the design.
- Text: explanatory text appears and transforms with user movement.
- Virtual objects: appear in space to connect diffuse objects.
- Wayfinding: created to guide users.

Based on our design studies, outputs proposed included a wide variety of displays (at a variety of scales), physical computing, and audio formats. There is likely to be a varied and changing set of outputs. Outputs that could be understood and displayed spatially were best suited to this setting. Those that require text output or auditory settings need careful consideration of location, unlike visual displays that can overlap without creating confusion.

When considering inputs, a critical distinction exists between afforded and interactive inputs. Afforded inputs are those that because of physical or cultural factors are understood without the need for visual feedback. By contrast, interactive inputs require more or less continuous feedback to be effective. They are largely based on text entry and editing and can be very difficult in spatial settings.

Equally important to specific affordances is the need to change the way that architectural space must be conceptualized and understood. The normative standards of architectural design, emphasizing geometric clarity, simplicity, or uniqueness, will be less important than how places connect with the meaningful activities of the users. For architects, programming human occupation is almost always understood as preliminary to the creation of form and geometry but for AR there is a greater importance of embodying users' actions as a variable within any project.

Moreover, it is important to note that creating architectural spaces with embedded AR interactions is a difficult task and requires more human-centered design and development. Creating interfaces in architectural settings requires more effort focused on usability studies and development, as well as more interoperability between architectural design software and this interface.

Obviously, in addition to architectural designers, many of the proposed interactions and designs require more substantial interdisciplinary work ranging from hardware design (to create more usable AR devices), data science (to understand and present data to users), software design (to create robust and scalable software), ethnography (to better understand human behavior), security (to make sure sensitive data is protected and secured), and ethics (to make sure designs are inclusive and non-infringing on user rights).

Unique architectural forms provided important and novel ways to engage with AR. One measure of this innovation is the surprising forms of the design solutions that would be difficult to understand without an appreciation of the possibilities of AR combined with spatial and architectural logic. In at least a provisional way, they provide a foretelling of the embodiment called for by Dourish and others.

If AR aims to create new forms of interactions that engage both technological and social factors, design methods must be able to represent both the architectural setting and information interaction simultaneously. This will involve expanding and transforming methods both in HCI and in architectural design; otherwise they will remain separate from each other and from the life of the places they occupy. This provides a great opportunity to create a unique approach. Embodied architecture takes advantage of AR for visualizing and collaborating during the design process.

Notes

1 Sutherland, Ivan E. "The ultimate display." In *Proceedings of the IFIP Congress*, vol. 2, pp. 506–508. 1965.
2 Frith, Jordan. *Smartphones as locative media*. John Wiley & Sons, 2018.
3 Farman, Jason. *Mobile interface theory: Embodied space and locative media*. Routledge, 2020.
4 Low, Peter. "'As a stone into a building': Metaphor and materiality in the main portal at Vézelay." *Word & Image* 22, no. 3 (2006): 260–267.

5 Köhler Ryan, R. "Toward an Anagogical Imagination: How Gothic Architecture Might Make Known the Things Unseen." Biennial Conference in Philosophy, Religion and Culture: The Expressible and the Inexpressible, 2012.
6 Watkin, David. *A history of western architecture*. Laurence King Publishing, 2005.
7 Bergdoll, Barry. *European architecture 1750–1890*. Oxford University Press, 2000, p. 77.
8 Kessler, Sarah. "This Company Built One of the World's Most Efficient Warehouses by Embracing Chaos." *Quartz*, December 19, 2017. Accessed July 25,2024.https://classic.qz.com/perfect-company-2/1172282/this-company-built-one-of-the-worlds-most-efficient-warehouses-by-embracing-chaos/.
9 Stoltz, Marie-Hélène, Vaggelis Giannikas, Duncan McFarlane, James Strachan, Jumyung Um, and Rengarajan Srinivasan. "Augmented reality in warehouse operations: opportunities and barriers." *IFAC-PapersOnLine* 50, no. 1 (2017): 12979–12984.
10 LACMA extension. OMA. https://www.oma.com/projects/lacma-extension.
11 Weiser, Mark. "The Computer for the 21st Century." *Scientific American* 265, no. 3 (1991): 94–105.
12 Poslad, Stefan. *Ubiquitous computing: smart devices, environments and interactions*. John Wiley & Sons, 2011.
13 Jacob, Robert, J.K. "Eye tracking in advanced interface design." *Virtual environments and advanced interface design* 258, no. 288 (1995): 2.
14 Greenberg, Saul, Nicolai Marquardt, Till Ballendat, Rob Diaz-Marino, and Miaosen Wang. "Proxemic interactions: the new ubicomp?." Interactions 18, no. 1 (2011): 42–50.
15 Hall, Edward Twitchell. The hidden dimension. Vol. 609. Anchor, 1966.
16 Buxton, William. "Living in augmented reality: Ubiquitous media and reactive environments." *Video mediated communication* (1997): 363–384.
17 Marquardt, Nicolai, and Saul Greenberg. *Proxemic interactions: From theory to practice*. Morgan & Claypool Publishers, 2015.
18 Dourish, Paul. *Where the action is: the foundations of embodied interaction*. MIT Press, 2001.
19 https://www.youtube.com/watch?v=SSC0RkJuBVw&ab_channel=Mrwhosetheboss.
20 https://www.youtube.com/watch?v=JjyJTCmpNH0&ab_channel=ACMSIGCHI.
21 https://kotaku.com/kishonna-gray-video-games-racism-consultant-pokemon-go-1850477275.
22 Azuma, R.T.: 1997, "A survey of augmented reality," *Presence: Teleoperators and Virtual Environments*, 6, 355–385.
23 Chi, H.-L., Kang, S.-C. and Wang, x.: 2013, Research trends and opportunities of augmented reality, *Automation in Construction*, 33, 116–122.
X. Wang and M. A. Schnabel (eds.): 2008, Mixed reality in architecture, design, and construction, Springer Science & Business Media.
24 Webster, A., Feiner, S., MacIntyre, B., Massic, W. and Krueger, T.: 1996, Augmented reality in architectural construction, inspection and renovation, *Proc. ASCE Third Congress on Computing in Civil Engineering*.
25 Bruce, T., Piekarski, W. and Gunther, B.: 1999, Using augmented reality to visualize architecture designs in an outdoor environment, *DCNet*, 1(4.2), 1–9.
26 Dunleavy, M.: 2014, Design principles for augmented reality learning, *TechTrends*, 58, 28.
27 Bolter, J.D., Engberg, M. and MacIntyre, B.: 2013, Media studies, mobile augmented reality, and interaction design, *Interactions*, 20, 36–45.

28 Bagdanov, Andrew D. "MNEMOSYNE: Enhancing the Museum Experience through Interactive Media and Visual Profiling." In *Multimedia for Cultural Heritage*, edited by Andrew D. Bagdanov, Alberto Del Bimbo, Lea Landucci, and Federico Pernici, 2011. Springer.
29 Shi, J. and Alt, F.: 2016, The Anonymous Audience Analyzer: Visualizing Audience Behavior in Public Space, *Proceedings of the 2016 CHI Conference*.
30 Webster, A., Feiner, S., MacIntyre, B., Massic, W. and Krueger, T.: 1996, Augmented reality in architectural construction, inspection and renovation, *Proc. ASCE Third Congress on Computing in Civil Engineering*.
31 This section of this chapter is a modified version of an already published paper by the authors:

Sauda, Eric, Alireza Karduni, and Noushin Radnia. "Architectural User Interface." in Co-creating the Future: Inclusion in and through Designe, edited by Burak Pak Gabriel Wurzer, and Rudi Stouffs, eCAADe, page 351–360.

The designs and quotes in this section are the result of a collaborative studio led by the authors in which different architectural designers presented their ideas. The quotes in this chapter are collected by the authors from the designers throughout the studio process.
32 Schön, Donald A. *The reflective practitioner: How professionals think in action*. Routledge, 2017.
33 Schön, Donald A. "The architectural studio as an exemplar of education for reflection-in-action." *Journal of architectural education* 38, no. 1 (1984): 2–9.
34 Poon, Josiah, and Mary Lou Maher. "Co-evolution and emergence in design." *Artificial Intelligence in Engineering* 11, no. 3 (1997): 319–327.
35 Gibson, Shimon, James Tabor, Rafael Y. Lewis, and Steve Patterson. "New Excavations on Mount Zion." *Ancient Jerusalem Revealed. Archaeological Discoveries* 2018 (1998): 304–313.

8

INTERACTION

Digital installations

In "The Medium is the Message" published in 1964, Marshall McLuhan argues for a particular understanding of media:

> The electric light is pure information. It is a medium without a message, as it were, unless it is used to spell out some verbal ad or name ... Whether the light is being used for brain surgery or night baseball is a matter of indifference ... This fact merely underlines the point that "the medium is the message" because it is the medium that shapes and controls the scale and form of human association and action.[1]
>
> (p. 23)

It is especially noteworthy that this example is specifically focused on the spatial aspects of the media, something that McLuhan often includes.

Within the fields of architecture and HCI, there has been enthusiasm for projects that incorporate forms of emergent technology into spatial settings, both in HCI as well as in design disciplines including art and architecture.

For example, video art dates back as far as the 1960s and includes Nam June Paik's *TV Budha*[2] 1974, a video sculpture by Nam June Paik featuring a Buddha statue watching an image of itself on a TV screen. The screen's image is produced by a live video camera trained on the Buddha statue. Bill Viola's *The Veiling*[3] 1995 images of a man and a woman are seen passing through nine panels of diaphanous cloth, slowly walking toward each other and merging at the center before moving away again into the night. Using slow motion, Viola gives visual form to time and the intersection of

DOI: 10.4324/9781003363392-8

male and female images. *The Veiling* explores both the individual's experience of self and our understanding of human interaction. Bruce Nauman's work *Live-Taped Video Corridor*[4] features two stacked television monitors at its far end, both linked to a camera mounted at the corridor's entrance: the top monitor plays live feed from the camera, while the bottom monitor plays pre-taped footage of the empty passageway from the identical angle. Walking down the corridor, one views oneself from behind; the camera's wide-angle lens heightens one's disorientation by speeding the rate of one's movement producing an unsettling self-conscious experience of doubling and displacement. All these examples are installed in specific spatial settings and use technology to destabilize and redefine the definition of art and media.

Interactive art and architecture

Computer-based interactive performance, art, and installation have become common in the last 30 years, and its history has been extensively studied by Steve Dixon.[5] He defines digital performance broadly and includes all work where computer technology plays a transformative rather than a subsidiary role. He is interested not in replacing existing technology with equivalent digital technology that is a bit cheaper, but rather in how digital technology makes possible work that was previously impossible. And he notes the centrality of the internet in the development of digital performance as an immense and readily available database but even more importantly as a method of collaboration and distribution. There is widely shared enthusiasm among digital artists and theorists for new possibilities offered by advanced uses of computation as a way to challenge and reinvigorate design and artistic practice. Lev Manovich is a chief provocateur for this, suggesting that the greatest artists today are computer scientists, and "the greatest hypertext is the Web itself, because it is more complex, unpredictable and dynamic than any novel that could have been written by a single human writer, even James Joyce" (p. 15).[6] This avant-garde attachment to the disruptive effect of technology is nearly universal among artists and theorists of new media. While Dixon notes the complete opposition from the knowing cynicism and cool distraction of postmodern art discourse, he rejects it on behalf of the artists that are his subject.

In the chapter entitled "Liquid Architectures and Site-Specific Fractures in Reality," Dixon most directly addresses digital architecture. First he identifies an "abstracted and fluid, yet physical form of space" based on renderings of imaginary spaces of the future. And second, he cites the Salt Water Pavilion by Nox Architects, the Fresh Water Pavilion by Lars Spuybroek, and the Guggenheim Museum in Bilbao by Gehry. These buildings have in common the use of NURBS-based modeling software creating complex curved surfaces, often obscuring canonical distinction between horizontal and vertical and leading to a shorthand description of "blobitecture."

Architects have become increasingly interested in the use of technology beyond just novel formal style by designing spaces that use technology to sense humans and react to their presence. The Bartlett Interactive Architecture Workshop, established in 1995, has continuously explored such endeavors by focusing on

> research that is predicated on the notion of architecture as time-based, changing its form and behaviour, rather than being static and fixed. As such, the people and objects in the built environment can be regarded as performers, especially where the behaviour of those objects is also subject to change over time.[7]

This definition, focusing on change of space over time driven by humans as actors within it, is not a novel rendition of spatial thinking. Doors, lamps, thermostats are all interactive elements of architectural settings and follow this logic. However, the design of such elements rarely occurs in the design of space. Thus, this view does challenge the predominant focus of architectural practice on static imagining and design of spaces. We are also interested in a method that is more than just a novel formal style; one that embeds HCI in the design of space, and allows architects to think about interactivity, a continuous back and forth interaction between actors and space driven by technology. For that we turn to the idea of precedents.

Precedents

For architects, the idea of a precedent is a central part in a student's education, allowing him or her to be able to understand previous buildings and use them as a model for current design. They are drawn using standard orthographic drawings (plans and sections) that allow variations of scale and geometry to be clearly understood. But they are rarely used (or at least discussed openly) after architects graduate and enter practice. Architectural monographs and lectures on current work seldom use precedents (other than an architect's own work) as an important part of their design presentation, unless the precedents are suitably vernacular or ancient enough to pose no threat to the originality of one's current work.

For HCI, a parallel idea to precedent is the discussion of related work (also known as a literature review) that is a requirement for research publications. It provides context, highlights flaws in previous research, identifies new methods, and highlights gaps. Such literature reviews demonstrate the explicitly collaborative nature of research in the field. Good literature reviews are typically not simply summaries of annotated bibliographies of current publications. Instead they are a generative explanation of important issues relevant to the current design that can connect a wide range of possible strategies including existing models with shortcomings, methods from other fields that may offer new procedures, and conceptual strategies from related disciplines.[8] The nature and methods of analytic description diagrams are critical factors in how we understand and conceptualize designs, something for which neither HCI nor architecture alone are complete, and which therefore requires a re-evaluation of the diagrams used to analyze precedents and propose new designs.

For interaction in architectural settings, orthographic projection such as plans and sections can precisely capture the spatial arrangement of elements over the entire environment. Unlike spatial diagrams sometimes used in HCI that describe only immediately adjacent surfaces (e.g. most AR applications), these also provide a holistic description of the organization of architecture, reminiscent of Gibson's environmental perception described in Chapter 6. However, while these diagrams can also be vital for construction and fabrication, they are much less effective at describing changes that happen over time.

Fortunately, diagrams including flowcharts and pseudocode from HCI describe the change of a system over time as more data are collected and processed. A pseudocode is a step-by-step description of an algorithm written in simple English rather than any programming language intended for human understanding and not machine reading. Flowcharts are diagrams describing a workflow or process where different shapes represent steps in programming such as data storage, if–then switches, and calculations. Unlike orthogonal representation such as sections or floor plans, both pseudocode and flowcharts change over time. They are also intended for use with large numbers of instances, rather than the one-off emphasis common in art and architecture. The weakness of this system is the lack of an overall spatial framework that organizes these settings.

Moreover, as we discussed in our earlier chapter on meaning, neither HCI nor architecture has a sophisticated methodology for dealing with people's behavior and meaning within a spatial setting. Architects assume that the building program that precedes their design captures the important aspects of a proposed building, but it is in fact often the result of economic imperatives or simplified descriptions of human organization. HCI designers often employ adapted ethnographic methods to explicitly study human behavior. But as Bell and Dourish[9] have noted, the goal is often reduced to a list of simplified "design factors" that lack the depth of understanding at the core of ethnography. One of the main reasons for the importance of our co-authorship with the anthropologist Dr. Lanclos is our common belief that this kind of thick description is critical to any non-trivial understanding of interaction.

Thus, a complete understanding of interactive settings must be a mixed set of diagrams and descriptions, in the same sense that we refer to mixed reality as a merging of a physical environment and a virtual one, for example in an AR system such as Hololens or Apple Vision. First, we need a *spatial layout* that describes the spatial structure using orthographic projection including an inventory of hardware technology that includes the apparatuses such as sensors, inputs, and outputs included in the system, indexed to the spatial diagram. We also need an *interaction diagram* using pseudocode that captures the unfolding over time of the algorithm in the setting, again indexed to the apparatuses. This will include separate registration for data and computation and an interaction counter to record how many people are engaged in each setting. An important criteria is a clear description of interactivity. Sheizf Rafaeli's contingency view identifies three levels:

- Not interactive, when a message or action is not related to previous messages or actions.
- Reactive, when a message or action is related only to an immediately previous message or action.
- Interactive, when a message is related to a number of previous messages or actions and to the relationship between them.[10]

A *thick description* as mentioned in Chapter 4 is needed to understand human interpretations of the setting, which currently relies on the published intentions of the designer as well as the reported reactions from users either directly or through reviewers or through the designer's self-reported observation of users. An important part of this diagram is the video. This is a tentative but as yet incomplete step toward a thick description of meaningful human behavior correlated with position and movement.

We surveyed 50 interactive installations gathering images, videos, and statements describing the intentions of the designer. Based on this preliminary survey, we selected a series of 11 for detailed studies that vary in terms of technology, scale, and interaction complexity. Our goal was to use this mixed set of diagrams to reveal significant differences within the medium of interactive installation.

Nervous Structure, Cuppetelli & Mendoza, Halifax, 2019

Spatial Layout

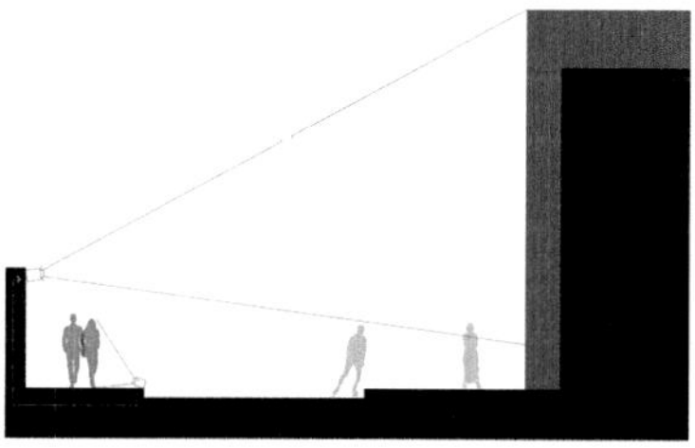

Interactions

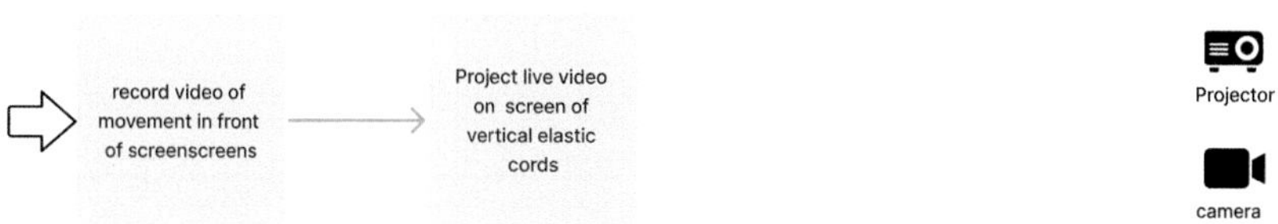

Thick description

real time video capture projected on moire screen...loose sense of connection between user's motion and final image...direct connection between screen and motion through installation

FIGURE 8.1 *Nervous Structure*, Cuppetelli and Mendoza, Halifax, 2019.

Nervous Structure, *Cuppetelli and Mendoza, Halifax, 2019*

Nervous Structure is an interactive installation composed of hundreds of vertical elastic lines illuminated with interactive computer graphics that react to the presence and motion of viewers. The piece consists of the intersection of the physical plane (the structure of elastic lines) with the virtual plane (the video projection of the visitor's motion). The artists' note that "our interest lies in the perceptual effects that arise from these intersections." These optical results of two overlapping grids that are not in perfect alignment is a moiré pattern, a term used widely in physics and computer graphics. These artists have done a number of installations varying in scale (from room wall size to entire building exterior) and setting (from inside to outside).

An understanding of the engagement with the visitors to these installations comes entirely from a series of brief videos. In all these cases, people easily grasp the effect that motion in front of a camera has on the moiré pattern. The processing and subsequent abstraction of the video image preserves privacy and encourages freedom of movement (singing of arms, jumping). The depth and variety of user engagement is limited by the simplicity of interaction.

The spatial location of this installation is central to its success, placing the screen of vertical lines in a position where it is public and very active. The large scale of the installation and the location near circulation is important to its creation of a public event. The interaction diagram is very simple, relying largely on the juxtaposition of the projected image with the fixed screen. The simple range of possible interactions limits the possibility of a thick description.

Volume, *United-Visual-Artist, V&A Museum, London, 2006–7*

Volume is a grid of 48 narrow, square, ten-foot-tall columns in an exterior courtyard standing in stark contrast to existing architectural or natural elements. Each column has speakers that present synth sounds and one face that consists of LEDs of a single color from bottom to top. Each column is equipped with proximity sensors, allowing it to respond individually to movement. The result is a direct response between an individual and a single column as well as a pattern of the interwoven paths of all the visitors. The Infra-Red (IR) illuminated scene is captured using a strategically placed camera, with an IR filter. People in the scene are tracked and then this information is fed through to a visualization system, which controls the LEDs.

To gain insights into visitor engagement, we conducted an in-depth interview with the artists and an art critic.[11] Walking up to a column

Volume, United-Visual-Artist,V&A Museum, London, 2006-7

Spatial Layout

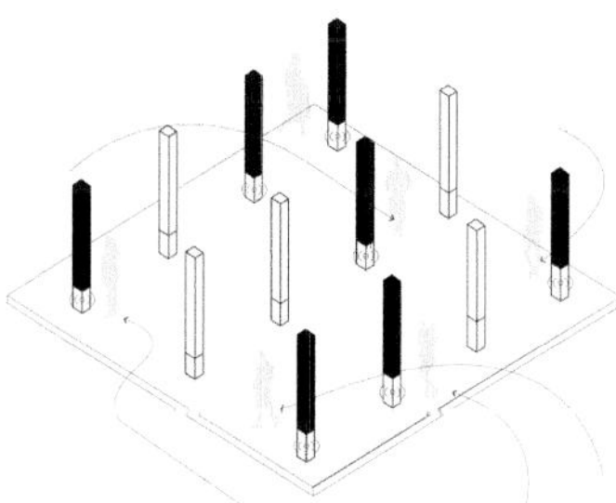

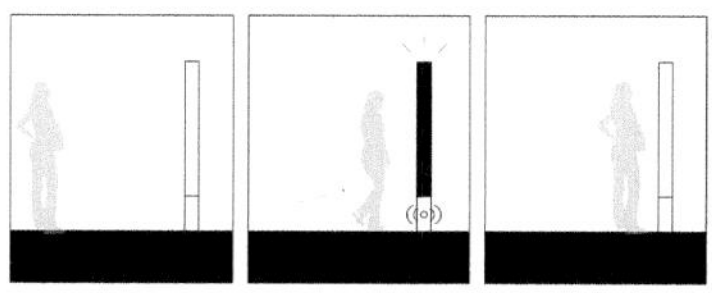

Interactions

1-24

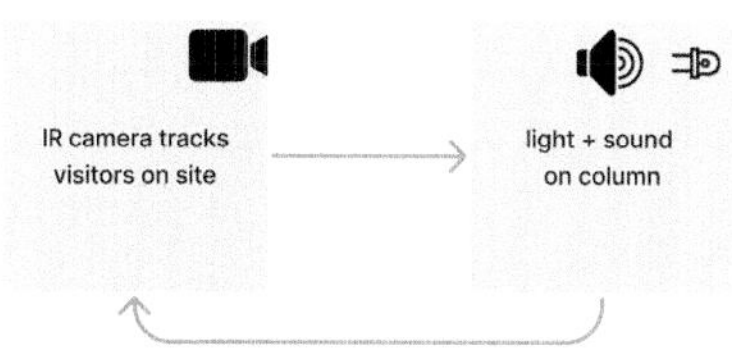

Thick description

can only detect relationship between movement and sound/light emissions when on one or two user are these...a general aura of activity is more typical...a diffused communicatiion with the installation

FIGURE 8.2 *Volume*, United-Visual-Artist, V&A Museum, London, 2006–2007.

activates its sound and light in an assertive manner. It is described as mesmerizing; visitors get very close to the columns and stare at them as if they were trying to work out how to communicate with them. As the number of visitors increases, the patterns of display are so complex that the connection to individual positions is harder to discern.

The space is clearly defined as a regular grid of simple geometry that contrasts with the existing courtyard. The interaction diagram is very simple; the sensing of the positions of humans in front of each column trigger the sound and light. Each column is triggered separately but the reaction of the 48 columns quickly become complex as more people join in. Discerning the impact of any single individual becomes challenging. A thick description of the effect is made difficult by this obscurity.

Bodies in Motion, *Todd Bracher and Studio, Milan, 2019*

Bodies in Motion is an immersive light installation created for Humanscale at Milan Design Week 2019. The installation is inspired by Humanscale's history as pioneers in human factors and natural ergonomics, bringing a scientific approach to furniture design. Situated in the warehouse of Ventura Centrale in Milan, the work features a minimal representation of the human body formed of lights that respond to the movements of visitors. As visitors' bodies are scanned, 15 motorized lights project tightly focused white beams onto a screen 15 meters away. The points of light on the screen map to key points of the person's body including the head, shoulders, elbows, hands, sternum, hips, knees, or feet. Each person that interacts triggers a specific visual and sound experience that is tightly synchronized across the two.

The spatial location is a prominent wall area upon which projections are made. The interaction diagram involves the projection in real-time, simplified, skeletal form captured by motion capture. The connection between the skeleton and a user's body is clear and it responds in real time. This affords visitors the chance to "dance" with the installation, moving back and forth and raising one's arms. The description remains very simple and reductive due to the limits of the interaction.

Boundary Function,[12] *Scott Snibbe, Wolfsburg, Germany, 1998*

Boundary Functions projects lines between each of the people walking upon its 4 m x 4 m floor. These lines demarcate each person's personal space: the space closer to him or her than to anyone else. As more and more people walk onto this floor, each person's tile changes dynamically to create an overall pattern mathematically described as a Voronoi diagram.

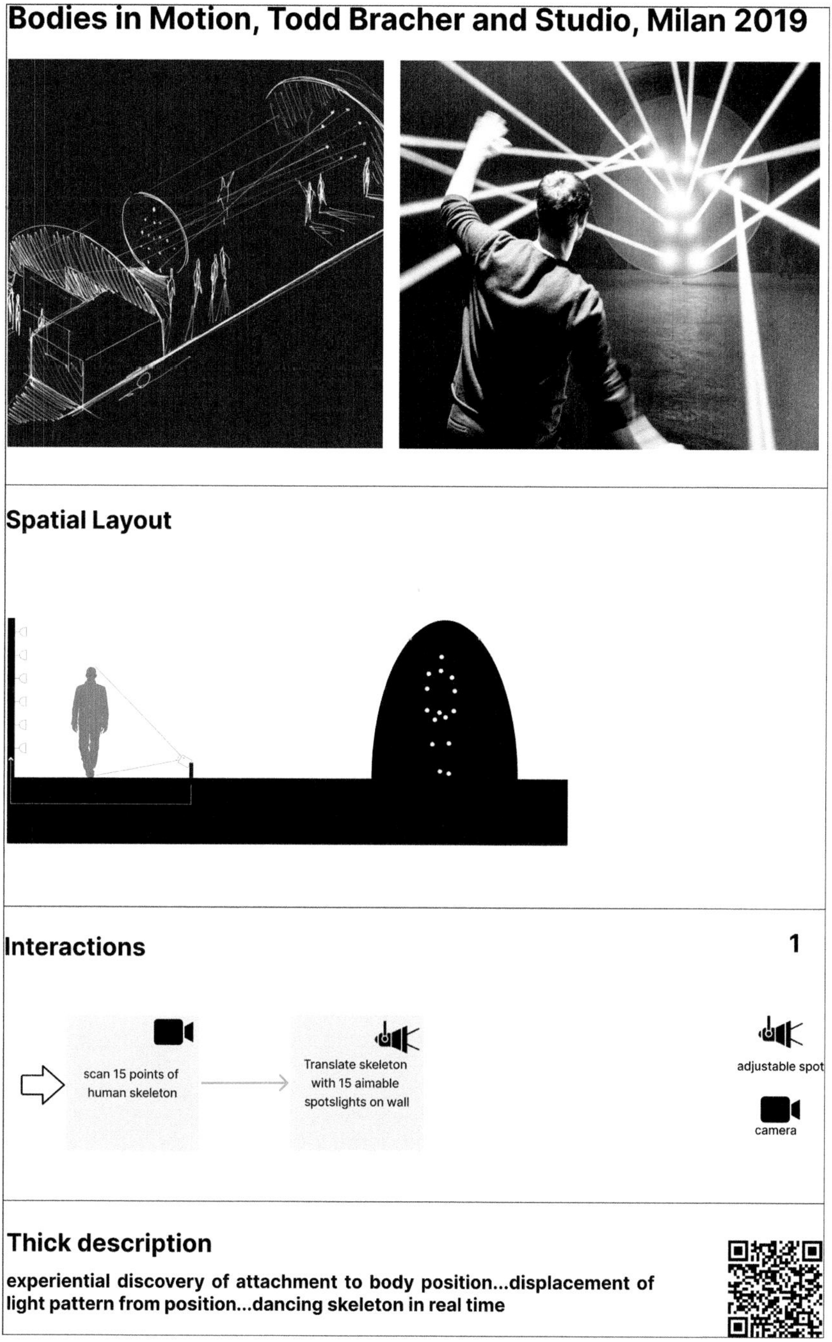

FIGURE 8.3 *Bodies in Motion*, Todd Bracher and the Green Eyl, Milan, 2019. Images courtesy of Todd Bracher and the Green Eyl.

Boundary Function, Scott Snibbe, Germany, 1998

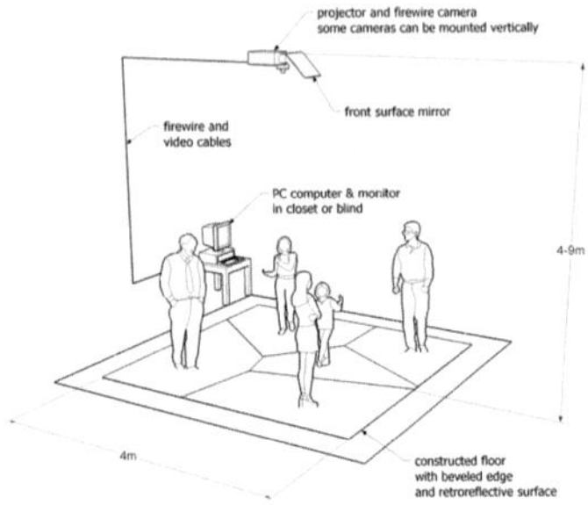

Spatial Layout

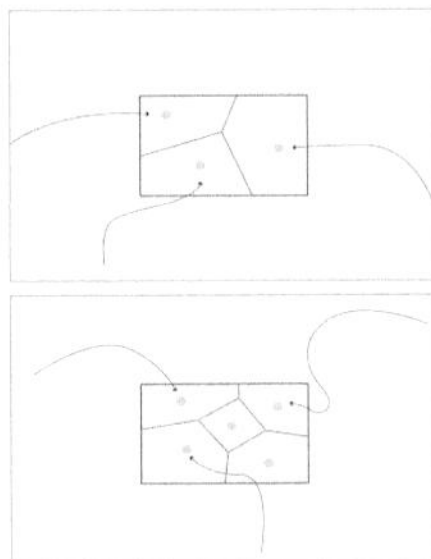

Interactions

2-5

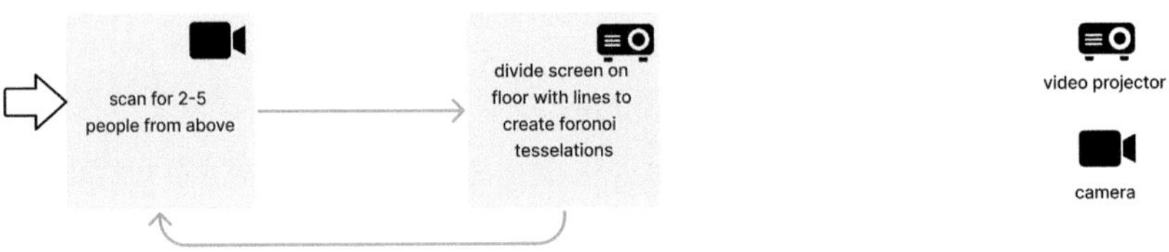

Thick description

immediate response to movement on the surface..almost a dance between the screen and the users... position speeds up and slows down..jump to different states when user enters of leaves

FIGURE 8.4 *Boundary Function*, Scott Snibbe, Wolfsburg, Germany, 1998.

This installation demonstrates the author's principles of social immersive media. The exhibit is visceral by responding to a user's movements and relationship to every other nearby body. The exhibit is responsive, updating in real time. It is continuously variable, changing continuously. It is socially scalable, becoming more complex as more people join. The exhibit is socially familiar by revealing our personal space. *Boundary Functions* often enlivens social interaction and provokes strangers to converse. It contains an educational message and has been included in exhibitions on mathematics, geometry, sociology, psychology, physics, and animal behavior. Children's museum planners have chosen this exhibit to create enthusiasm for a potentially dry topic.

The paper published as a result of this installation includes a detailed section concerning the engagement of visitors. People in different countries behave differently in the exhibit. In Germany, people move far from each other. In Japan, people immediately come close to each other and strangers even touch. In New York City, people stand on the floor and do not move. We believe these differences may be attributable to differences in cultural psychology. The narrative model of *Boundary Functions* is experiential. There is a continuous "reality" created by the exhibit whose behavior is predictable, yet continuously variable.

The space is located on the floor which is unusual for video projection. The interaction diagram is immediately responsive to the people who are tracked. It is understood as a tightly choreographed dance between the floor and the human. The description is very simplified, including only two to five people at once. The engagement of this installation is simplified to work with the technology, but builds only a limited connection with the users.

Pool, *Breakfast, New York, 2019*[13]

The collective BREAKFAST focuses on the physical computing elements of brixels and flip-discs which use stepper motors or magnets to pivot the rectangular brixels or the round flip discs. *Pool*, unveiled at Christie's in New York, reproduces reflective water movements as ripples across the horizontal surface. The whirl of sound and reflections of the surface generated by *Pool* create an engaging aesthetic visual and acoustic. The surface of *Pool* exhibits wave motion through the motion of the brixels along the surface and which persists for 20 seconds.

The spatial setting of *Pool* is a long flat horizontal surface that establishes a clear boundary. The level of the surface is at about waist level, suggesting a connection to the tactile surface of our hand. Interaction with *Pool* is

Pool, Breakfast, New York, 2019

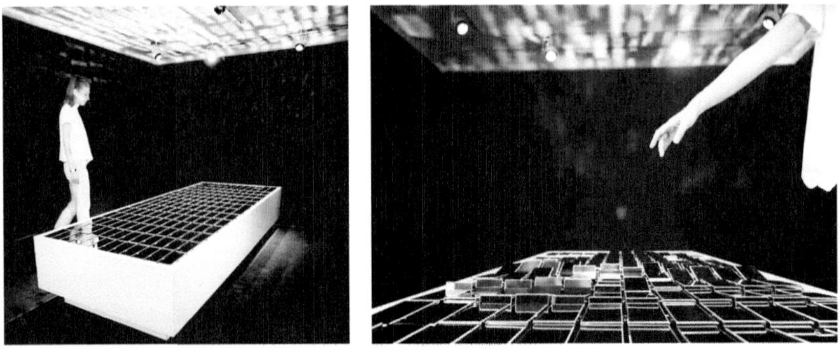

Spatial Layout

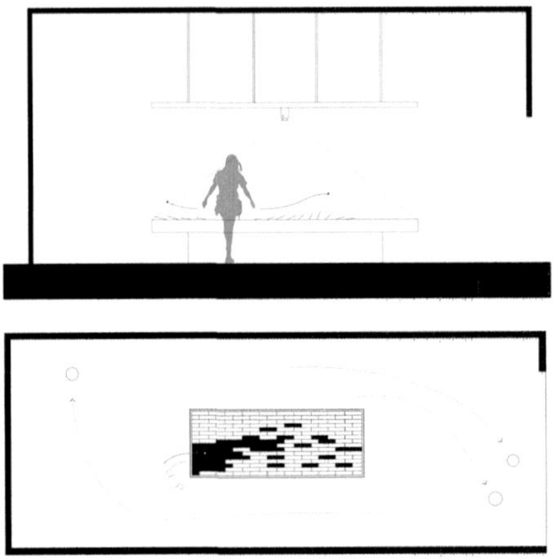

Interactions

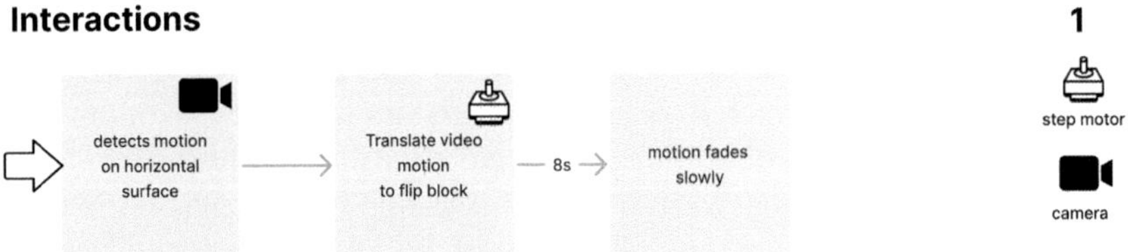

Thick description

response to horizontal movement...sound of wooden blocks making click/clack noise as they move...affordance of walking

FIGURE 8.5 *Pool*, BREAKFAST, New York, 2019. Image courtesy of the artist BREAKFAST.

engaged both by the sound of its operation, its motion over the surface, and its persistence over time. The description of the engagement is relatively thin, and may lose interest over time.

Harvard Time Capsule, also by BREAKFAST in 2020, is a similar installation that uses flip-discs to reflect one's movements in front of three wall-mounted sections. The video recording of motion is added to a database that is replayed as it slowly fades. It combines physical computing attributes with the persistence of delayed and repeated video.

D-Tower,[14] *Lars Spuybroek + Q.S. Serafijn, Doetinchem, Netherlands, 2004*

D-Tower is a permanent public art work that consists of a tower, a website that collects the emotional responses of the residents and changes the color of the tower in response, and a capsule under the tower to leave personal written responses. The unusual, 15-meter-tall, molded, epoxy structure has been compared to a Gothic vault and to the legs of a pony. A questionnaire is completed on the website every day by 50 people selected from the residents of the town. Based on an analysis of the responses, a color is selected (blue for happiness or red for love, green for hate, or yellow for fear). The *D-Tower* light comes on simultaneously with the street lighting. The answers to the questionnaires are then translated into "landscapes" shown on the website. The website www.d-toren.nl is still operating 20 years after the construction of the tower.

The engagement with this project operates primarily on two levels. First is the direct physical level of the unique tower both because of its form and its changing, symbolic color. Interaction with the tower is entirely indirect through the questionnaires on the website. Equally important is the engagement which allows for letters and comment-based dialogues about issues of common interest. An archive of these dialogues is maintained on the website.

The spatial location of the *D-Tower* is important in several ways. It is in the center of the town and it has a large amount of automobile traffic passing. It is placed in a park so that you can view it in the round from all sides. It is also a unique form: sculptural, curvilinear, and made of translucent fiberglass. The interaction diagram includes becoming present when the street lights illuminate at dusk. It also uses a website both for a daily poll and for others in the community to share ideas and thoughts. The thick description is limited mostly to this website while the tower itself does not contribute much to a deeper understanding.

D-Tower, Lars Spuybroek + Q.S. Serafijn, Doetinchem, Netherlands, 2004

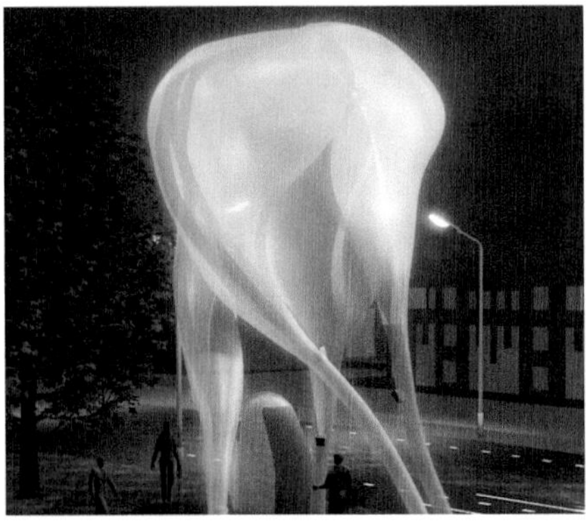

Spatial Layout

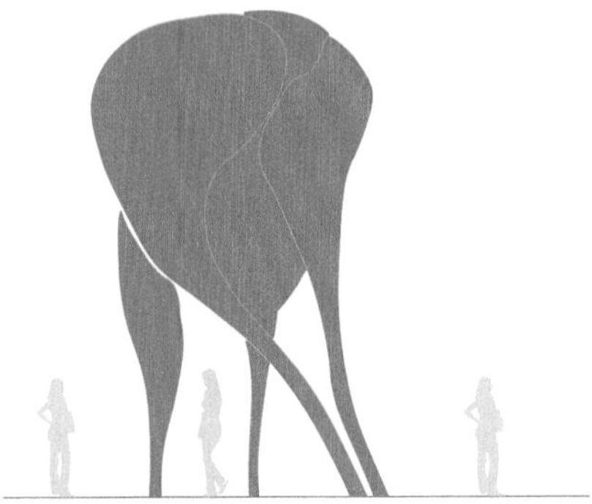

Interactions

50 (33,324)

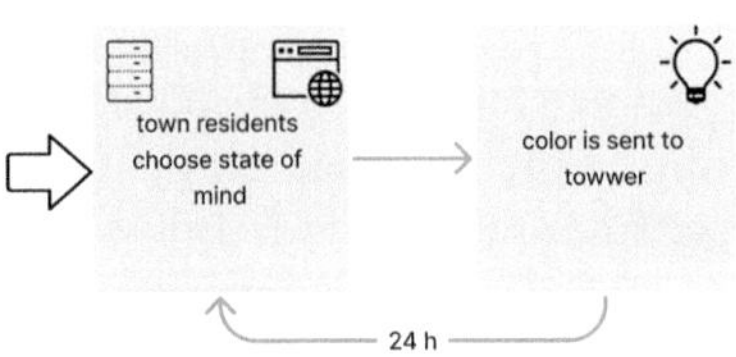

Thick description

anticipation of color every day at dusk..website as site for a texted base counterpoint to the simplicity of the tower color...unique form and structure of tower...twenty year history in the towm

FIGURE 8.6 *D-Tower*, Lars Spuybroek + Q.S. Serafijn, Doetinchem, Netherlands, 2004.

Access, Marie Sester. Ars Electronica, Linz, Austria, 2003

Spatial Layout

Interactions

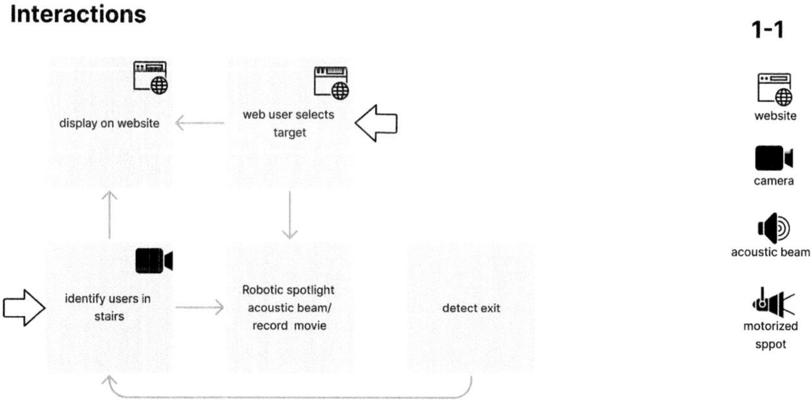

Thick description

engagement caused by motorized spotlight and acoustic beam...mystery of how a person is chosen (on website)..reaction of playfulness or avoidance

FIGURE 8.7 *Access*, Marie Sester, Ars Electronica, Linz, Austria, 2003.

Access,[15] *Marie Sester, Ars Electronica, Linz, Austria, 2003*

Access is an interactive art installation that applies web, computer, sound, and lighting technologies in which web users track individuals in public spaces with a unique robotic spotlight and acoustic beam system. A camera scanning the installation detects visitors and presents them on a remote website. Any visitor to the website can then select who to track next. The robotic spotlight automatically follows that individual while the acoustic beam projects audio that only that individual can hear. The tracking is active until he or she leaves the installation and a new person is chosen from the website. The tracked individuals do not know who is tracking them or why they are being tracked, nor are they aware of being the only persons among the public hearing the sound. The web users do not know that their actions trigger sound towards the target. The structure of *Access* is intentionally ambiguous, revealing the obsession/fascination for control, visibility, and vigilance: it can be scary or fun.

The engagement with this project solicits two distinct reactions. Some tracked individuals take pleasure in playing with the robotic equipment, jumping about in space and "daring" the machine to keep up. Others are horrified by the surveillance and seek to escape as quickly as possible.

The installation has been done in a number of spatial locations. It is always public, and was particularly effective in a location on a stair where engagement was sudden and surprising. The interaction diagram includes both direct engagement in the physical space and remote engagement through surveillance on a website. This creates a rich description that engages both a subjective and objective understanding of the installation.

Air Hugs, *Rachel Dickey, Charlotte, 2020*

Air Hugs[16] is a responsive environment activated by the color red, which receives, tracks, and moves with the passerby. A camera scans the installation, tracking a particular red hat worn by one visitor and subsequently activating the fans on that path, producing a gentle breathing and rustling sounds, and fields of reflection and light from the mylar material configured as lungs. The fans reverse and deflate the lungs as the hat moves on. When the large-scale inflatable lungs fill with air, they encase and enclose the space around the body, offering a deliberate, delicate, and gracious hug: Reasonable yet absurd, the title draws from the use of air as a primary material and the hug, which offers an immediate awareness of one's body and other bodies, and of the space between, or lack thereof, recalibrating human scale and enhancing social interactions.

Air Hugs, Rachel Dickey, Charlotte, 2020

Spatial Layout

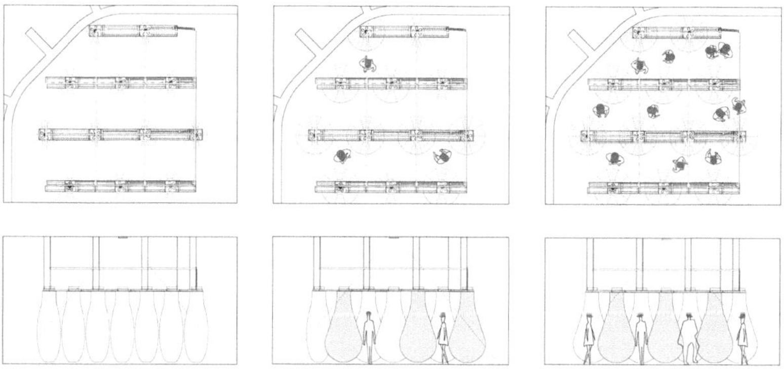

Interactions

1

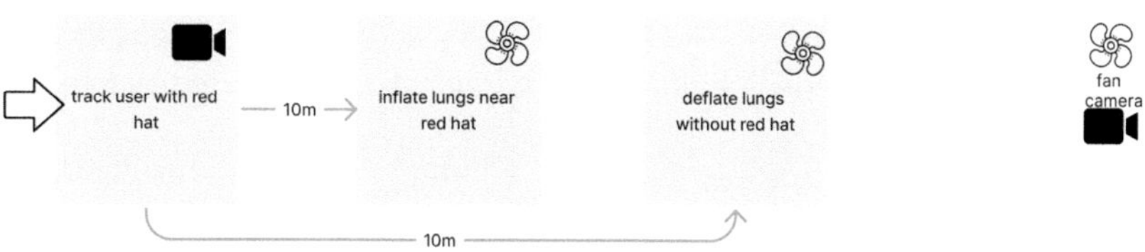

Thick description

sounds of fans and mylar inflating/ deflating... slow response to location of single person...uncertain response multiple users...strong architectural framework...Reflection of lights of moving mylar surface

FIGURE 8.8 *Air Hugs*, Rachel Dickey, Charlotte, 2020.

The engagement with this installation varies considerably with the number of visitors. With one or two visitors, the connection of the movement of the hat and the inflation and deflation can be understood. When the number of visitors increases, the general ambience of the rustling mylar, the ambient noise of the fans, and the lights and reflection from the lungs combine to create a layered tapestry.

The spatial location is defined by the enclosing art gallery as well as a strong three-dimensional framework of machines. The focused mechanical sounds of the machines enhance the center of the installation. The interaction diagram is very simple, a single sensor with complex results and little direct interactivity. A thick description in this installation is in contrast and loosely related to peoples' direct engagement.

Deep Walls, *Scott Snibbe, San Francisco, 2003 (12 other locations 2003–2008)*

With *Deep Walls*[17] users record silhouette movies by performing with their shadows in front of a projection screen. The duration of a performance is determined by their entrances and exits. When users walk in front of the projection screen, the exhibit begins to record their shadows. Upon the last user's exit, the resulting movie replaces the oldest of 16 cells projected in a grid. *Deep Walls* is an interactive wall that absorbs and "remembers" the acts taking place before it. People collaborate not only with other actors in front of the projector, but also with movies of previous visitors, in a recursive interaction loop. *Deep Walls* is visceral, engaging the body; it is responsive by replaying movies; is continuously variable; is socially scalable by accommodating groups; and is as socially familiar as a dance floor. *Deep Walls* is structured as an improvised performance narrative: both the users and the piece as a whole are constantly moving forward like an improvisational dance. The eventual erasure of each episode can cause people to strive to create a new performance that dramatically "comments" on the prior performances, or that re-enacts a performance that has disappeared.

We have a good source of information about the reaction to this work in a detailed review by an art critic. Users describe surprise and excitement in seeing what others have performed, sometimes engaging for hours. Despite the simplicity of this interaction technique – where all content comes from the users themselves – users sometimes engage with the piece for hours on end, and return to interact again and again over the course of years. People collaborate with movies of previous visitors, in a recursive loop, commenting on prior performances. Some recordings are an attempt to figure out the grammar of interaction. One installation has been used as

Deep Walls, Scott Snibbe, San Francisco, 2003 (12 other locations 2003 - 2008)

Spatial Layout

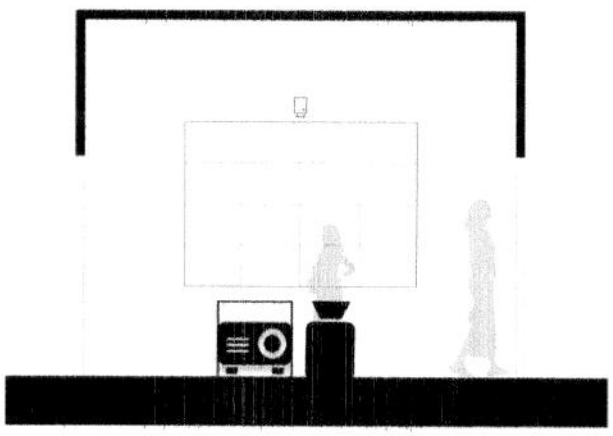

Interactions

1(16)

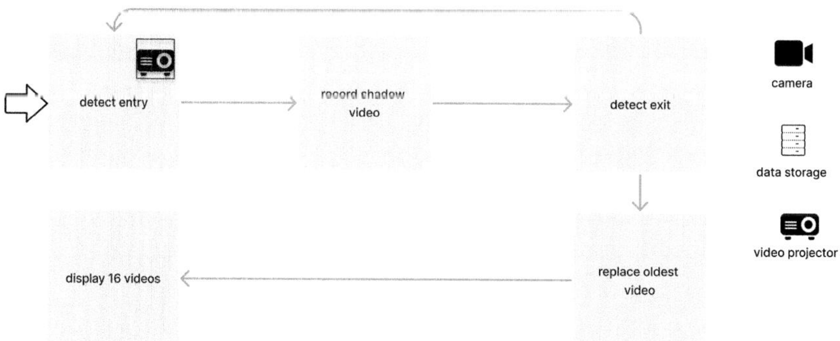

Thick description

casting shadow and comparing to recordings...ability to leave messages to observers...importance of wall as spatial setting...dnacing in front of the light

FIGURE 8.9 *Deep Walls*, Scott Snibbe, San Francisco, 2003 (12 other locations 2003–2008).

Mirrorspace, Roussel, Evans & Hansen, Paris, 2002

Spatial Layout

Interactions

1+1

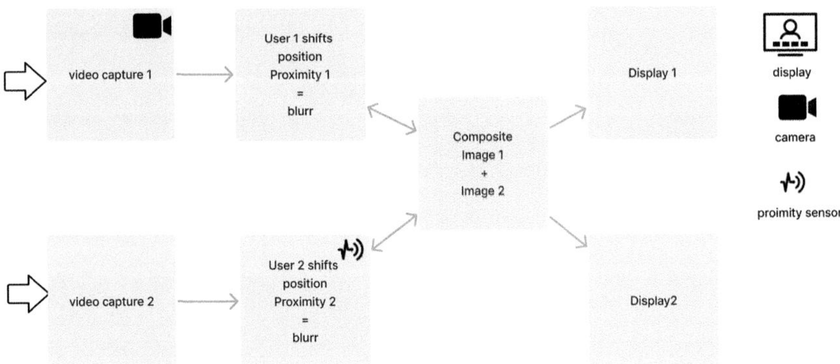

Thick description

mirror display changing as you approach...connection to another remote mirror display..ability to overlay ones own image with another user... changes over time ability to use as "game"

FIGURE 8.10 *Mirrorspace*, Roussel, Evans & Hansen, Paris, 2002.

a bulletin board, leaving visual messages; an exhibition's location influences interactions.

The spatial location is defined by the projection on the wall. The interaction diagram is legible for the user and connects to others. The rich description is defined by the ability to comments on previous users.

Mirrorspace,[18] *Roussel, Evans & Hansen, Paris, 2002*

Mirrorspace is a video system that uses proximity as an interface to provide smooth transition from visual awareness to intimate forms of communication. Roussel aims to create a language of physical proximity between people, similar to the work previously discussed by Greenburg on proxemic toolkits. *Mirrorspace* relies on the mirror metaphor, displaying images of the participants using a display screen, a camera in the center of the screen, and a proximity sensor. The important aspect is that two users engage simultaneously but not adjacent to each other. Each screen displays both the user in front of the screen and another, at first unknown, user. A blur filter is applied to express the distance of each image. This can be done in three ways: using the distance between people or using the added distances between people and their screen, or using the virtual relative distance between both people. Live streaming allows superimposition of two users that see their own reflection combined with a remote person and changes over time.

An installation was first created at an exhibition in the Grande Halle de la Villette creating a continuum of space that allows a variety of interaction. We have a record of the user relations from the designer, reporting first that the delays inherent in the early technology was not disturbing for users and that some even enjoyed it. All users reported that *Mirrorspace* was fun. Users reported feeling a sense of another person nearby, searching for other people in the space. There was some discomfort at how close other people could approach them on the monitor.

The spatial setting is not rigidly established, and evolves through the process of the users discovering each other. The archetypal spatial organization might have aspects of a maze that connects and disconnects. The interaction is complex and fluid between the users and allows exploration over time. Engagement with this installation offers potential for extension over multiple users and discoveries.

Roussel's expertise in HCI gives a particular focus to this project that while it is certainly an installation, also explores a wide and rich range of interaction.

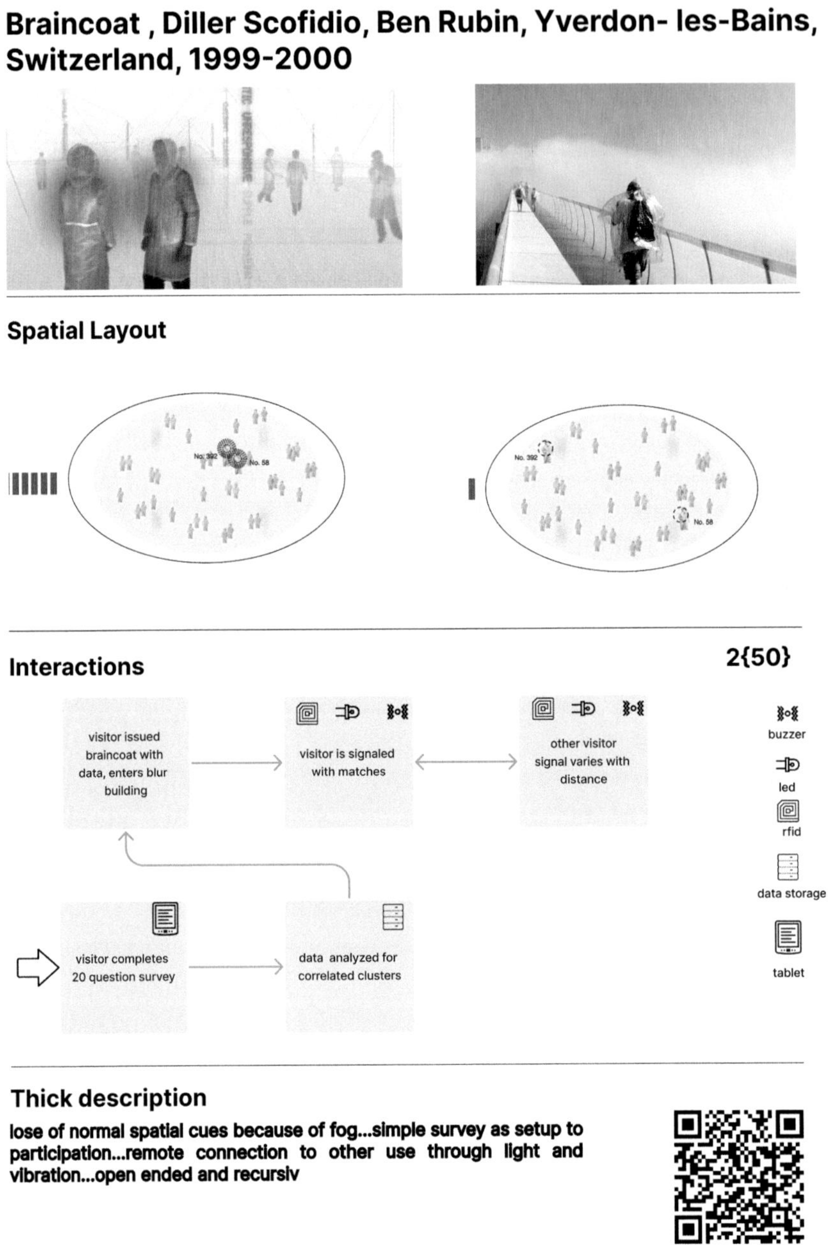

FIGURE 8.11 Braincoat, Diller Scofidio + Renfro, Ben Rubin, Yverdon-les-Bains, Switzerland, 1999–2000. © Diller Scofidio + Renfro.

Braincoat, Diller Scofidio, Ben Rubin, Yverdon-les-Bains, Switzerland, 1999–2000

The Blur Building was a temporary pavilion built for the Swiss EXPO 2002 by the architects Diller Scofidio + Renfro. Located at the base of Lake Neuchatel in Yverdon-les-Bains, Switzerland, the structure was intended to be an "architecture of atmosphere" or, as the subtitle of their book claims, "the making of nothing."

As part of this project, Diller and Scofidio were interested in a media project of some kind convening a think tank with consultants and Swiss communications companies. A number of alternative directions evolved for the technology and conceptual basis. Eventually, the idea of a Braincoat[19] was evolved as a smart raincoat that, in combination with a proxy communications network, creates a new form of "social radar." As the visitor in the fog environment is deprived of visual clues typically used to gauge the physical environment and social relations, the Braincoat acts as a prosthetic skin that receives and broadcasts signals. All visitors arrive at the LogIn station at the base of the Blur entrance ramp and fill in a questionnaire. The transceiver embedded in each braincoat has an imprint of the visitor's response profile that enables the coats to communicate in the fog. With the aid of a clustering program used for web profiling, visitors' profiles are compared and evaluated by establishing correlations among the range of questions. As visitors pass one another, their coats compare character profiles and create an involuntary reaction. The chest panel of the braincoat displays a diffused colored light, the color indicating the degree of affinity or antipathy, much like blushing from embarrassment or blanching from shock. The color range is coded so that a shift toward cool blue–green represents antipathy and a shift toward warm-red affinity. A small vibrating pad is located in the rear pockets. When two perfectly matched visitors encounter one another in the fog, a vibration excites the buttocks. Unfortunately, funding for this project was withdrawn before it could be completed, so we have no feedback about how this would have been engaged by users.

The space of the project was purposely indefinite. The only orientation available to people visiting was vertical and horizontal and perhaps swallowed or unswallowed. The interaction available was to be relative to others moving in Blur rather than an absolute measure. It is difficult to know how this would be received. Given the early states of communication technologies when this project was planned the background of the systems required too much customization.

The analysis of these precedents identifies strengths and weaknesses. Most of them establish a clear relationship to the architectural setting in

FIGURE 8.12 Brain Coat. © Diller Scofidio + Renfro.

which they occur. This can include the aggressively architectural stance of *Air Hugs* as well as the ironic, diaphanous presence of Blur/Braincoat, both of which are fully three dimensional. Others such as *Nervous Structure* and *Pool* establish a more simplistic relationship to a fragment of the settings such as a wall or a table; this provides a thinner description of interaction.

Another important distinction is the directness of the interaction, how immediately it is evident to the users. *Boundary Function* and *Access* provide immediate, real-time reaction to user movement, creating an almost dance-like interaction. Other installations such as *Volume* have a muddier reaction to movement and position, creating an atmospheric presence but only a general sense of user impact. An over-reliance of simple, direct interaction can limit engagement by users. *Deep Walls* is a special case that creates a direct interaction as well as echoing over time, establishing the possibility for a multi-user conversion.

Installations that are both immediately present and connected to web-based information demonstrate how interaction can operate on several modes and scales. *D-Tower* is an intentionally complex architectural form whose simplistic interaction is limited to once a day by an illumination color change determined by web poll. But the combination of *D-Tower* and a supporting website has continued for over 20 years to provide a rich menu for continued engagement. *Raincoat* uses both an interview by users and a direct interactivity between them on site as an engaging idea; the complexity of the implementation subverted the installation of this feature. *Mirrorspace* connects two monitors separated in space in an engaging way enabling two users to connect with each other.

The number of users engaged in an installation also varies widely. Some such as *Pool* and *Boundary Function* are very limited to two to five. On the other hand, *Braincoat* was meant to have a large number of users at the same time (perhaps 50 or more, though it was never completed. *D-Tower*'s simple interactive feature was meant to be created by a selected group of 50 residents and viewed by the 58,270 residents of Doetinchem. The implementation of large scale participation is not a developed feature of these installations, but is something that would be an inherent feature of a collaboration with HCI.

Notes

1 McLuhan, Marshall. "The medium is the message." In *Understanding media: The extensions of man*. MIT press, 1994. 23–35.
2 Mellencamp, Patricia. "The old and the new: Nam June Paik." *Art Journal* 54, no. 4 (1995): 41–47.
3 Iles, Chrissie. "Review: Bill Viola." Art Journal 54, no. 4 (Winter 1995): 97–99, 101. Accessed July 25, 2024. https://doi.org/10.2307/777706.

4 Barry, Melissa Marie. *The medium is the message: Bruce Nauman's films, videos, and video corridors, 1967–1970*. Texas Christian University, 2011.
5 Dixon, Steve. *Digital performance: a history of new media in theater, dance, performance art, and installation*. MIT press, 2015.
6 Manovich, Lev. "New Media from Borges to HTML." Introduction to The New Media Reader, edited by Noah Wardrip-Fruin and Nick Montfort, 13–25. Cambridge, MA: The MIT Press, 2003.
7 https://www.ucl.ac.uk/bartlett/architecture/research/bartlett-interactive-architecture-workshop-biaw.
8 AbuRa'ed, Ahmed, Horacio Saggion, Alexander Shvets, and Àlex Bravo. "Automatic related work section generation: experiments in scientific document abstracting." *Scientometrics* 125 (2020): 3159–3185.
9 Dourish, Paul, and Genevieve Bell. *Divining a digital future: Mess and mythology in ubiquitous computing*. MIT Press, 2011.
10 Rafaeli, Sheizf. "From new media to communication." *Sage annual review of communication research: Advancing communication science* 16, no. 1 (1988): 110–134.
11 https://www.polaine.com/2007/02/interview-with-united-visual-artists/.
12 Snibbe, Scott S., and Hayes S. Raffle. "Social immersive media: pursuing best practices for multi-user interactive camera/projector exhibits." In *Proceedings of the SIGCHI conference on human factors in computing systems*, pp. 1447–1456. 2009.
13 Silvia Iacovcich, "When sculpture transcends form, a view on new media artist collective BREAKFAST", *CLOT Magazine*, February 8, 2021.
14 Bullivant, Lucy. "D-Tower, NOX, Doetinchem, the Netherlands, 1998–2004 and Son-O-House, Son en Breugel, NOX, the Netherlands, 2000–2004." Architectural design 75, no. 1 (2005): 68–71.
15 Marie Sester. "Architecture du Paradis." Leonardo 34, no. 3 (2001): 186–186.
16 Dickey, Rachel. "Air hugs: a large-scale interactive installation." In ACM SIGGRAPH 2019 Art Gallery, pp. 1–6. 2019.
17 Simanowski, Roberto. "Scott Snibbe's DEEP WALLS: A Close Reading." *Dichtung Digital. Journal für Kunst und Kultur digitaler Medien* 8, no. 1 (2006): 1–6.
18 Roussel, Nicolas, Helen Evans, and Heiko Hansen. "MirrorSpace: using proximity as an interface to video-mediated communication." In Pervasive Computing: Second International Conference, PERVASIVE 2004, Linz/Vienna, Austria, April 21–23, 2004. Proceedings 2, pp. 345–350. Springer Berlin Heidelberg, 2004.
19 Diller, Elizabeth, Diana Murphy, and Ricardo Scofidio. *Blur: the making of nothing*. Harry N Abrams Incorporated, 2002.

9

CONCLUSION

Architectural user interface

In his book *The Structure of Scientific Revolutions*, Thomas Kuhn argues that the critical capacity for seeing a shifting paradigm is interpretive:

> Rather than being an interpreter, the scientist who embraces a new paradigm is like the man wearing inverting lenses. Confronting the same constellation of objects as before and knowing that he does so, he nevertheless finds them transformed through and through in many of their details.[1]
>
> (p. 122)

While we are not claiming that the paradigms we have been studying are as significant as those Kuhn referenced (e.g. the shift from Newtonian to Einsteinian physics), they demonstrate a similar resistance to change.

For contemporary computer science, human-computer interaction (HCI) has been a primary avenue of research. Areas of interest, including ubiquitous computing, design and creativity, the Internet of Things, tangible and embedded interaction, creativity and cognition, information visualization, and many others, are related to architecture. HCI and architecture have already begun to overlap in domain (the everyday built environment), in the use of design (as a method of exploration), and in engaging humans (as a central concern). While these overlaps provide interesting and possibly fruitful opportunities, they also conceal the very real differences between the disciplines. It is how these differences might be reimagined and how they might lead to a new hybrid that our research and this book has been focusing on.

DOI: 10.4324/9781003363392-9

During our research collaboration involving architects, computer scientists, and ethnographers working on augmented reality, computer vision, and interactive settings, we adopted the term "architecture user interface" as a shorthand description for a larger ambition that architecture should or even must be more than just a container for computing equipment. We had just witnessed the construction of a new academic building in an urban location that featured space for a 300-square-foot video wall facing out onto the street as a prominent feature near the entrance. It was included prominently in the building renderings and a five-foot-deep space and a generous budget were allocated for hardware and electronics. There was, however, no underlying idea about why it existed, how it would be programmed, who would program it, or how it would function as an interface. In the end, the space was used instead for a deep display window of academic bric-a-brac. The funding was eventually diverted to a roadside LED billboard sign at the main entrance to the campus (with all the same issues unresolved).

It is obvious that a number of technologies associated with computing were already deeply woven into architecture. This includes the laptop and desktop machines that are everywhere, but also the smart phones in every person's pocket and the Wi-Fi network in each building. In small buildings (homes and apartments) these may be relatively simple, but in educational, public, and large commercial buildings we might need to employ enterprise Wi-Fi systems with many zones and the ability to detect and track the location of people, devices, and assets. And the Internet of Things has resulted in thermostats, door bells, refrigerators, heating systems, and an exploding number of other devices connecting through Wi-Fi.

But beside an accumulation of technologies and devices, what might be the possibilities of an architectural user interface? This book is an attempt to provide, at least, a provisional answer.

Evidence of an architectural user interface

In the Introduction, we proposed a five-part hypothesis in this book. To reiterate, first, that the emergence of embodied interaction has drawn architecture and HCI closer together into a shared medium. Second, both disciplines will need to adapt; HCI by widening its scope and architecture by focusing less on the intentions of the designer and more on the user. Third, that ethnography understood as both a method and a theory is critical to creating a discourse between the disciplines. Fourth, that interaction in architecture can be defined ethnographically and understood by the position and movement of people within architectural settings. Fifth, that the nature of HCI is inherently concerned with thousands or even millions of points of data extending over long time frames that open unique opportunities for architecture. What evidence have we found that might point to an architectural user interface?

Movement is a unique input method for an architectural interface. From psychology, we have examined the way in which movement and position are critical to the perception of spatial information. Within architecture, circulation has always been a central organizing principle for design and occupation; the pivotal role of floor plans in architectural representation focuses on exactly these issues. Movement can be sensed by a range of technologies from motion sensors to Radio Frequency Identification (RFID) to camera-based computer vision. The precision, complexity, and security of these technologies vary greatly, but they can all be indexed to a common spatial representation.

A database of movement and position can be stored and be available as a basis for analysis over extended periods of time. Architecture has traditionally been considered finished with the completion of the construction of a building. There has been some work on post-occupancy evaluation, but this is a rare exception. Especially in healthcare design, demands are being made for change to improve the evaluation of the outcomes of procedures, and design prototypes used repeatedly in dispersed and complex hospital systems have evolved. By contrast, computer science usually deals with data collection over extensive locations or time. The emergence and advances of Geographical Information Systems (GIS) is a well-developed example that can serve as a model. Such databases can then be used to interpret and control a range of outputs from simple examples such as illumination and thermal comfort to more complex examples such as large-scale interactive displays.

A new description of the visual structure of building space can define the role that architecture has relative to HCI. The use of plans and sections are useful and necessary for the construction of a building as a tectonic object. The visual field described by Gibson in his work on driving and flight is one alternative system, but has never been developed for use in architecture. Another possibility is the work on space syntax by Hillier[2] which has been widely used in urban studies; one form of his analysis is directly relevant to the interior of buildings.

Buildings can be seen as a medium rather than as a static object. As we discussed in the previous chapter (Chapter 8), McLuhan cites the example of the electric light, which makes possible brain surgery and night baseball that deeply influence the media in terms of its scale, pace and pattern. To relate this directly to our work, we understand a medium to be inevitably connected to its architectural or spatial setting. But it also supports the idea of something that expresses itself over time and is made meaningful by the people who use it during their ongoing occupation of a building.

Any representation of an architectural user interface must include space, computing devices, interaction, and human meaning. The methods that are used by architects and by HCI researchers are very different from each other and neither are very tuned to movement or position. Using this hybrid analytic methodology would be a useful step in creating a richer, common understanding of a possible architecture user interface.

In contrast to the simplest and most obvious forms of interaction (e.g. an automatic door opener), context-aware computation includes both explicit and implicit acts of communication. Embedding computing into our lived activities requires minimal effort on our part and naturally fits our ongoing activities. It may not seem to be communication at all; rather, just normal activities.[3] Interaction is woven into everyday life.

The definitions of an interface and an interaction often vary from author to author and are sometimes used interchangeably. Dourish for example is clear that his interest is interaction as an activity rather than interface as a design. However, there may be some advantages to an interface as a design providing a coordinated set of concepts, hardware, and software that evolve over time but provide an ongoing framework. Two interfaces, for example, that have been remarkably resilient include the smart phone (uniquely defined by hand scale portability, voice input, location and inertial sensors, and small size screen) and the graphic user interface (defined by a desk sized screen, a keyboard input, graphic operating system, and a pointing device). The uses, advantages, abilities, and evolution of these interfaces were only partly predicted by the original design. The architectural user interface is not yet defined, but is likely to need to deal with multiple outputs to a variety of devices and an evolving definition of its embodied position in architecture. While it is possible to imagine text inputs using a keyboard or voice recognition, a building movement is better suited as an input method fitting seamlessly and unobtrusively into human activity.

Architectural user interface opportunity

An architectural user interface might offer the opportunity to understand behavior in architectural settings in a meaningful way over long time frames, including eventually the possibility of real-time understanding and response. It would also provide HCI with a richer understanding of the architectural setting and open new possibilities. Paul Dourish's interest[4] in "portholes" for distributed work groups is an early example of the role of physical context on interaction and leads to his more transformational work on embodied interaction.

How might this new ability change the way in which architectural settings are designed and analyzed? Simple interactive systems have a preset logic of response to the behavior of users, often limited by the capabilities of the display hardware and software. One description of an alternative "intelligent system" is the ability to identify and understand meaningful behavior and the ability to be programmed to act with a wide variety of responses.

An intelligent architectural setting would allow us to understand space in several new ways. First, we have the ability to get "hard" data on how human behavior is affected by the design strategy employed in a particular space. Designers have often used spatial and programmatic organizational strategies to justify experimentations in architectural form. For the first time we would be able to monitor the results of these experiments and evaluate their results. This offers us the possibility to create a broad analysis of design intentions; imagine a school design that can actually be analyzed for its ability to encourage positive and engaging behavior from its students and teachers, and that can be generalized over hundreds of design examples. Particularly those architectural sub-fields that build multiple instances of a common design would be able to learn from each new design and improve subsequent instances. We can also monitor how changes to a building, for example a hospital waiting room, affect the behaviors of the occupants. If a hospital were to reorganize the furniture in their waiting room, does that have an impact on the way in which users occupy the space? Do the users change the space on their own? How might we use this knowledge to make more useful and comfortable settings?

Second, there is the possibility of the development of real-time responsive environments, able to interpret behavior and suggest short term or immediately adaptive settings. Imagine an Alzheimer facility that is not just bricks and mortar but is able to track and understand the meaningful behaviors of the patients 24 hours a day, 365 days a year, understanding individual variation in behavior over both the short and the long term. For example, Alzheimer patients typically have trouble with spatial and visual issues, unable to distinguish between a shadow cast on the floor and a step. Intelligent architectural settings would be able to maintain observation of patients and understand the changes in his or her meaningful behavior. It could also be possible to predict what settings are likely to be difficult. This could be a flexible and programmable architectural setting that could become a part of the therapeutic setting, allowing adjustments to individual patient's therapy, creating an improved quality of life for the residents.

Venues

Christopher Morales, president of Freeman White architects, a prominent firm actively involved in medical and hospital design, proposed to his clients that they share data about the operation of their facilities (scheduling, staffing, etc.) when they began discussions about expanding their facilities:[5]

> With this data they could help make decisions that might help them understand how this data influenced the need for new or adopted facilities, or even the possibility of postponing building expansion. The obvious advantage was the partnership that would emerge in the long term. Despite some initial reservations about the strategy potentially limiting immediate design commissions, the resulting performance for those solutions that were informed by analytics and business operations far exceeded this limitation.

The likeliest venues for architecture user interface are those that have large public areas, established methods of gathering data about users, protocols about privacy, and ongoing architectural expansions and renovations. Besides medical facilities and hospitals this would also include large scale university research and classroom building, large scale retail and sports facilities, retirement, and nursing facilities (at a lesser scale but a more explicit need for gathering information and benign oversight).

For the technology industry aggressively developing new devices and software, the impulse is to maximize market share and profits. Amazon's Alexa virtual assistant technology using natural language processing has led to 600 million Alexa smart speakers located in buildings around the world. This huge number of listening devices, mostly in individual residential units, has arrived without any privacy controls, in contrast with the Health Insurance Portability and Accountability Act (HIPAA) Privacy Rule protecting medical information and health information. Bland assurance of their benign interests by Amazon, Facebook, or other enormous technology firms is not reassuring. Privacy concerns need to be addressed using a commonly accepted standard. Public spaces are the likeliest to have controls, but technology companies are likely to resist any limits.

As we have described in earlier chapters, there is likely to be considerable resistance to change from both architecture and HCI. With rare exceptions, architects are engaged professionally only for the period of the design and construction of a building. At both a financial level for quotidian firms and the demand for originality from "starchitects," the call for a long term commitment to organizations and their built environment will not be easy. For HCI researchers, the influence of architecture (i.e. spatial configurations) is understood as only a conditional factor. In planning egress routes, it would be certainly relevant in establishing the graph theoretical structure of the egress routing, but generally architecture is viewed as a dependent variable.

An important role may be needed for research collaborations between architecture, HCI, and ethnography. It is too early to know if disciplinary boundaries are too strong and the effort to find common ground too difficult. Architects may have to give up their roles as unfettered artists or the agents of narrow capitalist interests. They will need to demonstrate greater understanding of the social and political aspects that create architectural places as well as the role that computation can play as a coequal aspect of architectural settings. HCI may have to widen its perspective from a narrow interest in interaction to include the role of space and place as a wider context for human occupants. And it is worth remembering that ubiquitous computing suggests not a single new general use interface tightly connected to specific hardware but a number of interfaces adapted to different human settings. Important issues remain on how to understand settings that can be generalized and applied to a broader category such as architectural settings.

Establishing an architectural user interface is not inevitable and will not be easy. But the payoff for such a collaboration might be the emergence of an interface that is able to connect the wide understanding of architectural space, the modes of interaction afforded by computation, and the social creation of meaningful places.

Notes

1 Kuhn, Thomas S. *The structure of scientific revolutions*. University of Chicago press, 1997.
2 Hillier, Bill. *Space is the machine: A configurational theory of architecture*. Space Syntax, 2007.
3 Dourish, Paul. "Seeking a foundation for context-aware computing." *Human–Computer Interaction* 16, no. 2–4 (2001): 229–241.
4 Dourish, Paul, and Sara Bly. "Portholes: Supporting awareness in a distributed work group." In *Proceedings of the SIGCHI conference on Human factors in computing systems*, pp. 541–547. 1992.
5 Christopher Morales in conversation with the authors. As President of Freeman White, he created a research group at the firm with expertise in business administration, clinical nursing, and computer science to put this strategy in place.

BIBLIOGRAPHY

Alexander, C., 1977. *A pattern language: Towns, buildings, construction*. Oxford University Press.

Banham, R., 1980. *Theory and design in the first machine age*. MIT Press, p. 329.

Bell, G., and Dourish, P., 2014. *Diving a digital future: Mess and mythology*.

Beorkrem, C., Danilowicz, S., Sauda, E., Souvenir, R., Spurlock, S., and Lanclos, D., 2015. Keeping an eye out: Real time, real world modeling of behavior in health care settings. In: *Modelling behaviour: Design modelling symposium 2015*. Springer International Publishing, pp. 459–467.

Card, S.K., Mackinlay, J., and Scheiderman, B. 1999. *Readings in information visualization: Using vision to think*. Morgan Kaufmann.

Card, S.K., Moran, T.P., and Newell, A., 1983. *The psychology of human-computer interaction*. Lawrence Erlbaum.

Carpo, M., 2017. *The second digital turn: Design beyond intelligence*. MIT Press.

Clifford, J., and Marcus, G.E., eds., 1986. *Writing culture: the poetics and politics of ethnography: A School of American Research advanced seminar*. Univ of California Press.

Diller, E., Murphy, D., and Scofidio, R., 2002a. *Blur: The making of nothing*. Harry N Abrams Incorporated.

Diller, E., Scofidio, R., and Murphy, D., 2002b. *Blur: The making of nothing*. (No Title)

Dixon, S., 2015. *Digital performance: A history of new media in theater, dance, performance art, and installation*. MIT Press.

Dourish, P., and Bell, G., 2011. *Divining a digital future: Mess and mythology in ubiquitous computing*. MIT Press

Dourish, P., 2022. *The stuff of bits: An essay on the materialities of information*. MIT Press.

Dourish, P., 2001. *Where the action is*. Cambridge: MIT press.

Farman, J., 2020. *Mobile interface theory: Embodied space and locative media*. Routledge.

Geertz, C., 1974. "From the native's point of view": On the nature of anthropological understanding. *Bulletin of the American Academy of Arts and Sciences, 28*, pp. 26–45.
Geertz, C., 1973a. *The interpretation of cultures*. Vol. 5019. Basic books.
Geertz, C., 1973b. *Thick description*.
Gibson, J.J., and Crooks, L.E., 1938. A theoretical field-analysis of automobile-driving. *The American Journal of Psychology, 51* (3), pp. 453–471.
Gibson, J.J., 1950. *The perception of the visual world*.
Gibson, J.J., 1966. *The senses considered as perceptual systems*.
Gibson, J.J., 1979. *The ecological approach to visual perception*.
Gibson, J.J., 2014. *The ecological approach to visual perception: Classic edition*. Psychology Press.
Hillier, B., 2007a. *Space is the machine: A configurational theory of architecture*. Space Syntax.
Hillier, B., 2007b. *Space is the machine: A configurational theory of architecture*. Space Syntax.
Hutchins, E., 1995. *Cognition in the wild*. MIT press.
Kolarevic, B., ed. 2004. *Architecture in the digital age: design and manufacturing*. Taylor & Francis.
Kubo, M., and Prat, R. 2005. *Seattle public library, OMA/LMN*. (No Title).
Latour, B., 2005. Tapping lightly on Koolhaas's architecture with a blind person's cane… *Architecture d aujourd hui* 361, pp. 70–79.
Low, S.M., 2000. *On the plaza: The politics of public space and culture*. University of Texas Press.
Manovich, L., 2002. *The language of new media*. MIT press.
Marquardt, N., and Greenberg, S., 2015. *Proxemic interactions: From theory to practice*. Morgan & Claypool Publishers.
McLuhan, M., 1994. *Understanding media: The extensions of man*. MIT press.
Mitchell, W.J., 1996. *City of bits: Space, place, and the infobahn*. MIT press.
Mitchell, W.J., 1999. *e-topia: Urban Life, Jim# But Not As We Know It*. MIT press.
Mitchell, W.J., 2004. *Me++: The cyborg self and the networked city*. MIT Press.
Mitchell, W.J., 1990. *The logic of architecture: Design, computation, and cognition*. Cambridge, MA: MIT press.
Moravec, H., 1998. The senses have no future. *The Virtual Dimension: Architecture, Representation, and Crash Culture, 26*, pp. 84–95.
Norman, D., 2013. *The design of everyday things: Revised and expanded edition*. Basic books.
Oxman, R., 2006. Theory and design in the first digital age. *Design studies* 27 (3), pp. 229–265.
Pentland, A., et al. 2005. Human dynamics: Computation for organizations. *Pattern Recognition Letters*, 26 (4), pp. 503–511.
Picon, A., 2021. *The materiality of architecture*. U of Minnesota Press.
Rietveld, E., 2016. Situating the embodied mind in a landscape of standing affordances for living without chairs: materializing a philosophical worldview. *Sports Medicine*, 46 (7), pp. 927–932.
Schön, D.A., 2017. *The reflective practitioner: How professionals think in action*. Routledge.
Spurlock, S., Wu. H., and Souvenir, R., 2014. *Multi-view recognition using weighted view selection*. Asian Conference on Computer Vision, Springer International Publishing.

Sutherland, I.E., 1965. The ultimate display. *Proceedings of the IFIP Congress*, 2 (506–508), pp. 506–508.

Waber, B., 2013. *People analytics: How social sensing technology will transform business and what it tells us about the future of work*. FT Press.

Weiser, M., 1999. The computer for the 21st century. *ACM SIGMOBILE mobile computing and communications review*, 3 (3), pp. 3–11.

Winograd, T., ed. 1996. *Bringing design to software*. ACM.

Withagen, R., and Caljouw, S.R., 2017. Aldo van Eyck's playgrounds: Aesthetics, affordances, and creativity. *Frontiers in psychology*, 8, pp. 1130.

INDEX

Pages in *italics* refer to figures

For Product Safety Concerns and Information please contact our EU representative GPSR@taylorandfrancis.com Taylor & Francis Verlag GmbH, Kaufingerstraße 24, 80331 München, Germany

Batch number: 10711894

Printed by Printforce, the Netherlands